What You
DON'T KNOW
Can Keep You Out
of College

What You DON'T KNOW Can Keep You Out of College

A Top Consultant Explains the
13 *Fatal Application Mistakes*
and Why Character Is the Key to
College Admissions

BY Don Dunbar

WITH G.F. LICHTENBERG

GOTHAM BOOKS

GOTHAM BOOKS
Published by Penguin Group (USA) Inc.
375 Hudson Street, New York, New York 10014, U.S.A.
Penguin Group (Canada), 90 Eglinton Avenue East, Suite 700, Toronto, Ontario M4P 2Y3,
Canada (a division of Pearson Penguin Canada Inc.); Penguin Books Ltd, 80 Strand, London
WC2R 0RL, England; Penguin Ireland, 25 St Stephen's Green, Dublin 2, Ireland (a division
of Penguin Books Ltd); Penguin Group (Australia), 250 Camberwell Road, Camberwell,
Victoria 3124, Australia (a division of Pearson Australia Group Pty Ltd); Penguin Books India
Pvt Ltd, 11 Community Centre, Panchsheel Park, New Delhi–110 017, India; Penguin Group
(NZ), 67 Apollo Drive, Rosedale, North Shore 0745, Auckland, New Zealand (a division of
Pearson New Zealand Ltd); Penguin Books (South Africa) (Pty) Ltd, 24 Sturdee Avenue, Rose-
bank, Johannesburg 2196, South Africa

Penguin Books Ltd, Registered Offices: 80 Strand, London WC2R 0RL, England

Published by Gotham Books, a division of Penguin Group (USA) Inc.

First printing, July 2007
1 3 5 7 9 10 8 6 4 2

Gotham Books and the skyscraper logo are trademarks of Penguin Group (USA) Inc.

LIBRARY OF CONGRESS CATALOGING-IN-PUBLICATION DATA
Dunbar, Don.
What you don't know can keep you out of college : a top consultant explains the 13 fatal
application mistakes and why character is the key to college admissions / by Don Dunbar
with G.F. Lichtenberg.
p. cm.
ISBN 978-1-592-40302-8 (pbk.)
1. Universities and colleges—United States—Admission—Handbooks, manuals, etc.
2. College applications—United States—Handbooks, manuals, etc.
I. Lichtenberg, G.F. II. Title.
LB2351.2.D86 2007
378.1'610973—dc22

2007003926

Printed in the United States of America
Set in Trump Mediaeval and Trade Gothic
Designed by Judith Stagnitto Abbate/Abbate Design

*To my wife and best friend of forty years, Susan F. Finlay, M.D.,
a Dartmouth- and Harvard-trained and highly sought after
radiation oncologist, and our daughter Megan, a talented and
compassionate psychologist in faraway Oregon*

CONTENTS

Competition for colleges just keeps getting stiffer, but maybe that's hard to hear. After all, what good is knowing that back in 1932, nearly three quarters of applicants to Yale got in, while today it's down to thirteen percent? Why dwell on the fact that when you apply to one of the fifty or so most competitive colleges in the country, there are two, three, or even four other applicants whose scores, grades, and extracurriculars are just as impressive as yours, and you are all competing for one spot? It's not as if there are secrets you can learn to dramatically improve your chances.

Actually, there are. I've been helping applicants get into their dream schools for thirty years, and I've learned a secret I want to share. Of course, you already know that standardized tests matter. And you know how important your school record is: the grade point average along with a well-selected list of courses, the teacher recommendation letters, and the "brag sheet" of extracurricular activities. If the admissions office door has four locks on it, the first two keys are test scores and school record, and the third is special talent or some special accomplishment or quality. What is the fourth key?

It's "character." An old-fashioned word, it means the way you develop your inner qualities: intellectual passion, maturity, social conscience, concern for the community, tolerance, inclusiveness.

Do these qualities really matter to admissions committees? Yes. When admissions officers see a high SAT score, they ask, what sort of person got that score? When they read about students in leadership positions, they want to know, what sort of leaders were they?

You may be surprised to hear that character can matter as much to an admissions committee as test scores or school record, but as I've learned, if you don't demonstrate good character, you're as good as dead. Those who show they have it can beat out others who rank higher in GPA, test scores, and extracurricular achievement. Those who don't may do themselves in, no matter how good they look on paper. (Even if you have triple 800s on the Reasoning Test [SAT 1], perfect scores—and let's face it, you probably don't—your chance of rejection from Harvard is still a strong possibility.)

How do I know? When I was a guidance counselor for high school students at Andover in the early 1980s, I sat in with the college admissions committees as they made their decisions. Not just one admissions committee, but the committees of many of the most competitive schools, Harvard, Yale, and Princeton included. I listened as they read aloud from score reports and transcripts, from student essays and teacher recommendation letters. I heard them give their reactions and share their acceptances and rejections on the spot.

That's not how it works anymore. Independent school counselors rarely, if ever, sit in and listen, and I think it's because colleges now see this as favoritism, left over from a past era in which the preponderance of good candidates came from private schools. Back then, colleges knew more about who they were getting. Now, colleges do everything they can to be sure that public school kids compete on a level playing field. In the early 1980s, I learned through close observation and interaction exactly how admissions people thought and still think now. As a result, I identified personal mistakes that make all the difference. That knowledge is the basis for the success of my company, Dunbar Educational Consultants, which helps students from across America, as well as in Asia and Europe, to get into the best possible colleges for them. We visit colleges regularly to keep up with what they're looking for in potential students.

Of course, a lot has changed since the 1980s, but the values these institutions are looking for in their students have remained constant. Now more than ever, they are looking for students with character.

My goal is to encourage you to identify with the kind of character colleges want and demonstrate that character in your application. In this sense, I'm offering you an edge over the competition. When my company first started, a college counselor at one of the top New England boarding schools told me that she'd feel uneasy being in my shoes, "giving away all our secrets." At the same time, Ted Sizer, head of school at Andover when I was there, urged me to share with the public what I had learned from being on the inside. Up to now, I've only shared that knowledge piecemeal with our clients. In this book, I make my "secrets" available to anyone and everyone, not just to those who hire my company.

From thirty years of experience helping applicants get into college, I offer you these essential facts:

1. Character can matter as much as anything to an admissions committee.

2. Most people—including students, teachers, parents, and counselors—don't understand all that admissions people mean by *character,* or why colleges care about it so much.

3. Character matters no matter how strong your application may be. No matter who you are, you will be compared to other applicants with similar qualifications. So whether you're a math whiz or a Native American or a varsity swimmer, you'll be compared to others in the same "pool." That is, your application will be compared to that of other math whizzes or Native Americans or varsity swimmers. From then on, you no longer compete against all the other applicants to the college. For the most part, you only compete against the others in that pool. That can be a big advantage, but within your pool, students will probably look more or less alike on paper. (In the football pool, everyone's a

recruited football player, and so forth.) So you still need to show excellent character in order to stand out within your pool and be selected.

One article in *The New Yorker* promised to explain "why college admissions has become unpredictable." Even some professional counselors will tell you, "It's a crapshoot." But listen: It's no crapshoot. It's a matter of learning to recognize and avoid a list of predictable mistakes.

Who needs to worry about these character mistakes? These days, almost everyone. If you're applying to any of the top fifty schools, you can't afford to have a single glitch in your application. But no matter where you're applying, the competition has only increased, so the more flaws you can recognize and overcome, the better your chances will be.

How can there be fatal mistakes that your friends and your parents and your school guidance counselor don't know about? Because these are mistakes that only matter to a specific group of people: people trying to run a college. If you're not running a college, they might seem small, even invisible, at least at first. Here, for example, is the first sentence of a disastrous personal statement, written by an A-student who looked great on paper until he killed his college hopes with his essay: *"At my highly regarded private school, I am being prepared to excel at a superior college, which will hopefully bring me success and happiness in the future."* In this one sentence, an experienced admissions officer can quickly spot at least seven potentially fatal flaws. How many did you find?

At the end of this book, we'll review the mistakes in that disaster of an essay opening, and you can test whether you've learned to see them for yourself.

CHAPTER ONE

FATAL MISTAKE #1

You Don't Know What "Prepared" Really Means

Beware this error if . . .

—*You've been known to procrastinate, especially on big assignments*

—*You do your best writing at the last minute*

—*You usually make a good impression, so you figure you'll pretty much wing it on the interviews*

You'd be amazed at how many stories I've heard like the following one.

Bob's mother called me the day after early applications were due. "He doesn't want to show me his personal essay," she said. "He says he didn't even start writing until the night before the deadline and then he got sick of everything he had to say. So he just sent in whatever he had! He doesn't even remember if he ran spell-check. Are we in trouble?"

Yes, Bob's application was in trouble indeed. If the application season is a race, then Bob had collapsed on the ground with the finish line in sight. When I hear a story like this one, what I hear is not laziness. It's not exhaustion or an "understandable" feeling of being overwhelmed. What I hear is a lack of preparation.

Not that I blame anyone who runs out of time or patience for a college application. The fact is, no one is naturally prepared for this process, which asks you, as a high school student, to do things you would normally never choose for yourself.

Chatting with a strange adult you may never see again about your future (aka the Interview).

Documenting your high school life on preprinted forms, to be read by more strangers, most of whom you will never meet (aka the Application).

Waiting outside an all-night post office in the middle of winter, clutching envelopes that need postmarks (aka the Last-Minute Deadline).

These strange rituals of college application don't come naturally to anyone. You need to prepare, but that's not news. What you haven't heard, I'll bet, is what *prepared* really means. Most of all, being prepared means pacing yourself, making smart decisions about when and how you will work on your application *before* you ever sit down to write an essay, or fill in a short-answer question, or meet with an interviewer.

There are two aspects to keep in mind when pacing yourself, and they may sound contradictory:

Your application is a long race like a marathon.

Your application goes by in a flash.

How can this be? It may sound impossible that your application is both of these things at once, so let me explain what I mean.

PACE YOURSELF (Part One): YOUR APPLICATION IS A MARATHON

Half of mastering the college application process is recognizing just how long and challenging it will be. The first of several standardized tests may begin sophomore year with the PSATs. But from the point of view of your transcript, the process starts even earlier, as early as the end of eighth grade, when you pick your ninth-grade courses. After adding up the time spent on tests, meetings, essay drafts, campus visits, and just plain waiting, most seniors would agree that the application process lasts, on average . . . nine thousand years.

No wonder Bob felt sick of it by the end.

The trick to pacing, whether you're a marathon runner or a college applicant, is not to push yourself too hard. You could probably walk for hours, all day if you had to, but you can only sprint for minutes. Why? Because when you walk you naturally find a sustainable pace, one that doesn't leave you out of breath or build up lactic acid in your muscles. In the same way, I suggest you work on college applications at a walking pace, a comfortable pace. Of course, if you're going to do that, you need to plan out your time.

1. **Get started early.** Send for applications during spring of your junior year. (For quicker results, download applications from the colleges' Web sites.) These are usually ready by mid-July. In the meantime, even before then, you can at least download the Common Application.

   Once the school year ends, it's time to begin filling them out. Will you feel like it? Probably not. You may feel as if you'd rather have cavities filled. So make it easy on yourself. Commit to one hour each weekend. Just one hour.

That first day, just fill in all the nitty-gritty, obvious stuff. Put in your name, address, phone numbers. Get all of that factual information entered. I don't care if you're watching television while you do it. Just do it—easiest parts first.

Start making a list of activities for your "brag sheet." This is the list of all your extracurricular activities. You may find you don't remember everything at first. Put down all you can think of, then add to it as more comes back to you. For now, put down everything you've done. You can always cut the list down later.

2. **Commit to one work session a week.** Which is more productive at the gym: working out for forty minutes three times a week for three months, or working out for twenty-four uninterrupted hours without a break? Either way, it's the same number of hours, but the first approach could get you into shape while the second approach could kill you. In the same way, trying to cram in all of your application work right before the deadline could wear you out like poor Bob, but working steadily once a week throughout the summer will put you in a good position for the fall and winter. So commit to one work session per weekend, always at the same time. (Or if you know that you're more productive during the week, then pick the time of the week that feels best for you. But pick a time and commit to it.)

3. **If you miss a week, don't give up.** When I tell an applicant to work an hour every summer weekend, I expect that he or she will miss a couple. That's all right, as long as you get back to it the next week.

4. **Once you have the factual information filled out, start trying out ideas for the personal essay.** In Appendix A: "Writing the

Essay," I describe in more detail how to pace yourself while writing essays and short-answer questions. If you can write a first draft of your personal essay by following this once-a-week method, then the rest of the application will feel easier.

Of course, most applicants don't work this way. Many rely on a dangerous motivational technique. They wait until their backs are up against a deadline, and then they use fear to push themselves through the unpleasant work. You might say that this crisis approach has three parts:

1. Avoidance
2. Panic
3. Mad rush to the finish

Sound familiar? It's a popular approach. But why? First of all, it gives you something to do with your anxiety. If you deny how new and nerve-wracking this experience can be, then you channel all that anxious energy into racing for the deadline. Second, it makes a long, slow, and sometimes (let's face it) boring process into something rushed and exciting.

The trouble with procrastination as an approach is that rushing leads to sloppy, incomplete work. No one can maintain a sprint all the way through a college application, and when you rush, you tend to make careless mistakes, like leaving out part of the application, repeating yourself in different essays, or missing deadlines. Your thinking, too, becomes messy and immature. You think much better, more clearly, when you give yourself time to think.

"So all right," you may be thinking. "I get it. The challenge of the application process is that it's long, very long, like a marathon, so I need to learn some techniques to pace myself. This way I'll have something left over at the end, when it counts most, and I can finish strong."

PACE YOURSELF (Part Two):
YOUR APPLICATION GOES BY
IN A FLASH

How can a marathon go by in a flash? It all depends on your point of view. To you, the application process may move as slowly as a glacier, but to admissions people you go by like the wind. How can that be? Imagine looking through a telescope at the moon. When you look the normal way (into the eyepiece, of course), the telescope makes everything look bigger. But if you turn it around and look in the other end, everything looks smaller. It's the same moon and the same telescope, but depending on your perspective the moon can look either big or small. Which perspective is correct? Is the moon really big or really small?

Well, of course, the moon really is huge, so huge its gravity pulls on the oceans and makes the tides on Earth. But when viewed from Earth, it appears so small that you could hold up your thumb and blot it out. In a similar way, when you look for the finish line through the "telescope" of the admissions process, it seems very far away. But when admissions people see you through their end of the "telescope," they don't see the long journey and all the time and work and heart you put in. The "you" they see is in the form of an envelope with some pieces of paper in it, some computerized test reports, plus a short conversation or two. While you measure the application process in years, they measure your application in minutes.

The average application gets about twenty-five minutes of reading time—that is, if the candidate's record warrants a complete reading. One admissions person at Yale said that she could read fifty applications in a night. She probably gave twenty minutes to a kid who looked like he was a good candidate, and in her notes suggested to the two other readers to "look at this one carefully." A reader of your personal essay—provided you're in the ballpark academically—will likely give it three to five minutes. From this point of view, the application goes by very, very quickly.

To be successful, you need to

reach admissions people in ways that can fit inside their brief reading experience. What may feel endless to you is over in a flash for them, and that affects how they get to know you—if they ever do. Consider the example of Alison. From the start of the application process, Alison was nervous about getting teacher recommendation letters. Shy since girlhood, she was concerned that her class participation wasn't memorable. Would her teachers have enough to say about her? She knew that this was one of the biggest challenges for her as an applicant, so she allowed extra time for it. She started thinking about which teachers to ask during her junior year, and when a history teacher loved her term paper, she immediately asked that teacher to write a recommendation.

The history teacher wrote the letter and kept it on file until Alison began to apply to schools. She sent it to Alison's first-choice college, where it did exactly what we hope a letter will do. It made her stand out as a distinctive and interesting applicant with a real talent for thinking—in her case, for thinking about history. When Alison showed up for her interview, the interviewer had read about the term paper, and he asked to hear more about it. How had she chosen her topic and approach? Why did she think the paper had been a success? By then, it had been several months since she'd written the paper. At that moment, taken by surprise and under pressure to speak to a stranger, Alison couldn't remember much about what she'd written. "I don't know," she said. "I guess it just sort of worked out. . . ." The interviewer was excited to get to know her as a scholar, but to him she seemed withdrawn and unenthusiastic. Later he reported that she "didn't really seem to care about academics."

After the interview, she remembered more about what she'd written. And when she got home, she even dug out the paper and reread it, remembering how excited she'd been to find she had something she cared about saying. But by then it was too late to impress the interviewer. He had only one quick chance to get to know her, and what he saw was a shy girl who didn't even seem excited about her best work. She didn't seem to him like a particularly appealing student. To the interviewer, it was as if she'd never done all that fine preparation.

Maybe this sounds unfair. After all, Alison had done good work, and she had paced herself very well when it came to compensating for her shyness with an excellent teacher letter. Yet in the interview, she missed the chance to show the good work she had done. To me, there are few things more unfortunate than a hardworking applicant who misunderstands what it means to prepare for interviews and essays and winds up dangerously unready for her big moment. This situation also shows why admissions people sometimes wish the process were longer. If an interviewer were more like a teacher, a counselor, a parent, or a friend, he or she would have more time to get to know an applicant. But because there are so many applications, each one only gets very limited attention.

So what might Alison have done differently? She might have thought through the kinds of questions that her interviewer might ask her, making sure she was ready with examples fresh in mind. She could have reviewed some of the schoolwork she was most proud of (specific papers or books read or notes from classes she enjoyed participating in), so that when her interviewers asked her what she liked best in school, she had some specific examples ready for her brief chance to talk about herself. If she had been able to share her enthusiasm for writing about history, she could have made a very different impression on her interviewer and on the admissions committee as a whole.

Alison appeared to be suffering from Fatal Mistake #3, a lack of intellectual passion, which I'll expand on later in Chapter Three, but that wasn't the real problem. Alison loved her history class, she just wasn't prepared to talk about it when her brief chance came.

What They Want to Know About: You

These two mistakes of preparation—not pacing yourself for how long the process will feel to you and not preparing for how short it is from the admissions side—are not always separate in the minds of admissions people. To Alison's interviewer, it probably wasn't clear

---

INTERVIEW FIRST AID: *What if you forget?*

What if you're in an interview and you can't remember some specific detail about your schoolwork that the interviewer seems interested in?

Remember that an interview is not an academic test. If you can't remember the facts, you can still talk about your feelings for the class, how immersed you got in a certain project, how exciting it was to be so completely engaged, and what it made you feel about the subject matter in general.

---

whether she was an unmotivated student, a poor interviewee, or both. Often, admissions people don't have time to make these kinds of distinctions. In the same way, the readers of Bob's essay (the one he worked on for only a night) may not have known if it was sloppy and confusing because he had rushed, or because he was a sloppy and confused person, or because he didn't care enough about their college to do a better job. They may have seen his lack of preparation as a sign of other character problems: arrogance, selfish disregard for the people who read the applications, and so on. Poor Bob, tired and unprepared to talk about himself, might have seemed on paper like the sort of selfish student no college wants to have around. That's another example of how not being prepared becomes a deadly mistake.

Bob and Alison have something in common. At a crucial moment, they were both unprepared to talk about themselves. The results were fatal, because the kinds of questions colleges ask are not like the questions you're asked in school. They are questions about you, what sort of person you are and what you will be like at their college. The best college applications aren't just a record of the kind of student you *were* in high school, they are a creative projection of whom you *will be* in college. The good news is, the answers are all inside of you, but it takes time to recognize them and grow comfortable sharing them.

For this reason, too, I encourage regular, manageable work on the application. It's not just that working steadily, in manageable doses,

STEPS TO SUCCESS

B e prepared for the ways applying is too long *and* for the ways it's too short.

- Pace yourself, because *applying will feel very long to you.*
- Show admissions people that you are prepared to answer their big questions, because *your application is going to seem very short for them.*

How?

- Start early.
- Work in regular, short, unhorrible sessions.
- Remember that what they most want to know about is you, what you care about and what motivates you.
- So make who you are count.

will make you do better work, although that's true. Working steadily is actually easier than cramming and rushing at the end. This is what most people don't realize, as they slip into procrastination: It's actually easier to start early. If you have seven months, it's better to work for part of every month than to save your work until it feels pressing. Whether you have seven weeks or seven days or seven hours, it's still better to divide up your time. This is one of the secrets of the most successful students and the most successful performers in all fields. Start practicing way ahead of time and work regularly; don't try to do heroic amounts of work all at once. It's less painful and more fun. Ideas come more easily. You do better and feel more confident, because when you keep showing up to do the work, the best in you shows up.

CHAPTER TWO

FATAL MISTAKE #2

Just Being Yourself

Beware this error if . . .

—*You've been known to have your "immature moments"*
—*You're spontaneous and impulsive*
—*You believe honesty is the best policy, no matter what*
—*You only want a college that will take you "the way you are"*

It's probably the most common advice given to college applicants: *Be yourself. Let them see who you really are.* That may sound like good advice, but let me tell you, it could be the worst thing you ever do for your application.

Are you shocked? People often are. Once when I was on the *Today* show, an experienced and good guidance counselor challenged me: "Why don't you just let kids be themselves?" Kids should be allowed to be spontaneous, he said. That way they will be "more real" and "true to themselves."

Now, he had a point about authenticity. College interviewers want to get a feel for the real person behind your test scores and grades, the human being who will spend four years on their campus. So, yes, I want you to be as genuine, as relaxed, as true to your own voice as you can be. It's admissions poison to sound like a robot, droning out canned ideas. "Just being yourself" can be the antidote that loosens you up, letting you tap into your spontaneous, creative, and authentic side. And so we hear this advice over and over: *Be natural. Speak from the heart. Be yourself.*

My question is, which self? In an interview and in your essays, you certainly want to demonstrate your best self—showing your unselfish, intellectual, confident, socially caring side.

Let me give an example. When I was a high school teacher, I had a student for two classes during the same semester. His name was David. In one of the classes, which met in the afternoon, he spoke up often, and he helped make that period a pleasure. He was focused, energetic, and full of helpful contributions and real insights. I couldn't have been more impressed with him, and I considered myself lucky to have him in my class. (I would have been glad to say as much in a recommendation letter, by the way.)

The other class met at seven-fifty in the morning, and in that class, David seemed like a different person. Honestly, he seemed more like a zombie. He straggled in at the last possible minute and took a chair in the back corner. Some days he kept on his coat, and slouched down into it, until it looked like a blanket he'd pulled up to his chin. Was he actually asleep? I don't think so, but he didn't look all that awake, and he had little to say. He still did pretty well on tests, but other than that, I might have forgotten he was there. And so I started to wonder: Which one was the real David? The sparkling contributor or the withdrawn lump?

The answer, of course, was that both selves were real, both ways David could be. And it wasn't just David. Look around your high school, study it like an extraterrestrial scientist who wants to learn about humans, and you'll observe kids acting mature and immature, informed and clueless, selfish and generous, involved and bored, and so on. If you pay attention and you keep watching, you'll see the same kids do some of both. We all have a variety of selves, good, bad, and indifferent.

As the poet Walt Whitman wrote, "I contain multitudes." So, yes, it's good advice to "be yourself," your genuine self, not some manufactured impersonation of what you think the college must want. Still, the question remains: *Which of your selves will you choose to show?*

CAN'T YOU JUST BE HONEST?

Maybe you feel uncomfortable selecting among your "selves." Many people do. "Isn't it enough," I'm often asked, "just to be true to yourself? Isn't it enough to be honest?" I remember one student, a top high school athlete who had received a "likely" letter from an Ivy League school, meaning that as a recruited athlete she was virtually assured of getting in. (I explain how the process works, involving coaches, in Chapter Eleven.) She attended a presentation by that college where applicants were advised that what mattered most in the essays was their ability to "speak from the heart." And so she did. She decided it would be best to write about her regret that she hadn't worked harder in high school, and to explain that she would change when she got to college. Her heartfelt confession of her flaws as a student began like this:

> In high school years, I relied on my inborn abilities. The truth is, I studied very little. Other kids worked hard, but I felt like a slacker, coasting on natural intelligence or maybe even just good luck. I don't know exactly, but I felt like I didn't have to earn my grades, like most kids did. . . .
>
> I know it's terrible that I didn't challenge myself more, and believe me, I feel bad about it. When I get to your college, I'm going to turn over a new leaf. A whole new tree! I'm going to work hard at my courses and do some real learning and show that I deserve everything I get.

Were colleges impressed with her honesty? Apparently not. She lost her likely status and had to settle for her fourth-choice school. Why?

Because the personal statement is your chance to *select* an aspect of yourself to share with the admissions committee, a side of you that is distinctive. It's your chance to show what is truly special about you, not merely what is true. In this student's honest confession, colleges heard this: *Here's what you really need to know about me: I may be a strong athlete, but intellectually I'm a slacker, and even though I believed that slacking off was wrong, I didn't do anything to make it better. Bottom line, I don't work, not even for what I believe in.*

When confronted about the damaging subject of her essay, this was her answer: "It put me in a bad light, but it's true. And to say something otherwise would be dishonest."

I understand that when you're learning the art of presenting yourself, you don't want to compromise your integrity. I admire that impulse, but you don't have to view honesty in simplistic black-and-white, either-or terms. So I asked her: In all of high school, did you ever feel challenged? Did you ever have to work at anything? Did you ever work hard for something you believed was right? As we e-mailed and talked about it, she began to paint me a picture that was still honest, but more complicated. Some classes and assignments came very easily to her, but there were others that didn't. She had more than one story to tell. Even so, she resisted giving up her original topic. It was still true, she said, or it was one of the things that were true. Shouldn't she tell the truth?

AN APPLICATION IS AN AUDITION

I told her: Imagine you are going to audition for a role in a musical. You might know a thousand songs, but at the audition, you only get to perform one. Maybe two. Now, if you want to be completely honest, you might tell the musical director that there are some songs you sing terribly. They're out of your range, you don't really like them, they make you sound unconvincing, and you can't motivate yourself to practice them. You could even perform that one nightmare song, the one that sends listeners running from the room, holding their ears and laughing.

But you won't. You'll consider the songs that show off the talents and skills the director needs, and then pick one of those you can sing really well. You'll be honest—you won't try to lip-sync to a recording of a stronger singer—but you'll show off what you've got. You'll be honest, but choosy. You have to decide which of your selves, which honest aspects of your personality, to feature.

WHAT IS YOUR "BEST SELF"?

When I talk about your best self, I mean the side of you that is best suited to the college experience. The side of you that is most excited about learning. The side that is mature, open-minded, energized, unselfish, confident, and caring about your fellow students and your school—in other words, what you're like when you are most able to rise above the fatal mistakes described in this book. Of course, admissions people understand that you're not at your best every moment of the day. They're not either. But just as a talent scout hopes to see you perform as well as you can, they want to see the best you've got.

Consider my experience with my drowsy student, David. As his teacher, I had the chance to get to know him over two class periods a day, five days a week, for an entire semester. You could say I got to hear him sing a lot of his material. In time I learned that his morning slug-

REVISING THE RULE

~~Just be yourself.~~
Show them your best self.

gishness was a problem he was gradually learning to solve. I discovered that his family was going through a difficult time, and he was often on the phone until late at night, talking through some challenging emotions. His true self was the active class participant. As his teacher, I had the luxury of getting to know him over time, but admissions officers don't have the luxury of time. They just get their one quick chance to form an impression. You have to be prepared to show the side of yourself you want them to see.

The combination of not knowing how to select the sides of yourself to show and not having much time to show admissions people who you are can be very dangerous. Imagine that during this same semester, David arrives for an early morning interview at his first-choice college. As he takes off his coat, his eyelids are heavy. Beneath his jacket and tie, he can feel his shoulders wanting to slouch, and his back itching to slump down deep in his chair. Still, he tries to stay focused. He shakes the interviewer's hand, and he takes a seat. The interviewer starts off with some chitchat.

"Are you enjoying this year at school?"

"Sure," David says.

"What's something you especially enjoy?"

David has not prepared for a question like this, so he thinks about what he'd enjoy right then. He reaches down into himself and says something genuine and honest.

"Sleep," he says. It's not what he meant to say, but he's nervous and tired and he hasn't been on many interviews, so out it comes.

"Excuse me?" the interviewer asks.

"Sleep. You know. I always feel better when I get a good night's sleep. This semester I had a seven-fifty class, and it just about killed me. All I could think about was how good it would feel to close my eyes."

The interviewer nods. She has only this brief chance to meet David, and unless he recovers quickly, she'll never get to hear about any of his other, more compelling selves. David has been honest, genuine, spontaneous—and also shortsighted and immature. Of course, immaturity is a genuine part of David. Maybe it's a part of us all. But schools want to hear the best you've got, and part of being your best self is having the maturity to keep some sides of yourself under wraps, when necessary. Interviewers don't expect to see fully developed adult maturity, because you aren't a fully developed adult. The point is to give them the chance to see your potential. But David hasn't done that, and at this school, David will forever be remembered as the kid who'd rather sleep than go to class.

HOW CAN YOU RECOGNIZE YOUR BEST SELF?

It's so important to use your brief chance to introduce yourself well and to reveal the sides of yourself that could be meaningful to colleges. Many of the fatal mistakes in this book are simply missed chances to develop and show those sides. But before we get to the chapters on the specific sides of yourself you need to show, I'd like to define *best self*. What makes the best sides of yourself "best"? Is there some checkup you can give yourself, when you're working on your application or meeting with a teacher, counselor, or interviewer, to know if you're showing your best self?

In order to understand the most common, basic mistakes, let's look at the stories of a few more unfortunate applicants who did themselves in by "just being themselves."

INTERVIEW FIRST AID

It's one thing to know in your mind that you want to show your mature side, but what do you do when you blurt out something totally inappropriate or immature?

Acknowledge the mistake, then immediately try again. Show your self-awareness by saying, "I guess that came out sounding a little off, but what I meant to say was . . ."

Show What Distinguishes You

One generally strong candidate, Stephen, advised to just be himself, decided this meant he should be true to his own impulses and feelings. With unabashed enthusiasm, he wrote in his personal statement: "My first priority in choosing a college is the school's prestige, especially its reputation among Wall Street recruiters. Your excellence will enable me to position myself for the job market and business school."

Despite generally high grades and impressive test scores, Stephen was rejected at his top choices. Why? There are several reasons why this was an unsuccessful approach, and we'll return to the subject in more depth in later chapters, but the most basic flaw is that he didn't show his readers anything distinctive that they cared about. He was completely out for himself and offered not one thought about contributing to the college or learning out of interest. He appeared Machiavellian. His essay boiled down to this: *I want to come to your college because I'm hoping to have lots of success.* And the admissions people replied, Well, who isn't? Don't everyone's priorities include success? He might as well have written, "There's nothing special about me. I'm just an ordinary selfish person, looking out for number one." You may find his attitude bracingly honest or you may find it depressingly self-serving, but either way, what he showed of himself was utterly ordinary. He sang the most overplayed song in the book. This was a student who had many impressive, interesting characteristics that he could have written about equally honestly, showing his drive for success but also presenting the unique individual who was driven to become a valuable person. Unfortunately for him, the colleges never got to know that side of him.

Show Your Adult Side

Another student, Tom, got caught up in his fondness for bathroom, bodily-function humor. He wrote his essay in the form of a review of

Tom's International Encyclopedia of Fart Jokes, a blog he was compiling daily on his personal Web site. His camp counselor was a big fan of the blog, which he regarded as "extremely funny." Now, I can understand that tastes vary and that humor is a great way to let off steam, especially at a stressful time like college application season. But the jokes in this essay just didn't say "college applicant." They said "seventh-grader." They screamed it. And with the exception of his camp counselor, I think that few other adult readers would have imagined admissions people could share the humor. Tom gave the impression that even his best self was too immature for college. I strongly encouraged him to find another essay topic.

Go Beyond Yourself

Brenda's interviewer began with a little small talk, pointing out that Brenda looked like she'd gotten some sun recently. The interviewer's remark broke the ice, and Brenda started to talk about her trip:

> Oh, yeah, I went to the Caribbean. I'd lay out on the beach, and feel the sun, so relaxing. . . . Mmm. And there was this band there, playing on the beach. These guys were really cool, and they'd play all day long, but singing in French, you know? And I thought it sounded really beautiful. Every

---

FIRST AID: *Humor*

Humor is a great way to connect with people, if they laugh. If they don't laugh, it can be a disaster, as bad as writing IMMATURE in red letters across your application. If you're trying for humor in an essay, test it out on some adults—and not just the pushover who always laughs at your jokes. Find an objective and mature adult to be your guinea pig.

morning I had my coffee in bowls instead of cups or mugs, which I just thought was so cute, and I dipped a baguette in it. I think French bread is the best bread in the world, don't you? And people say the food in the islands isn't that good, but this one restaurant was like the best dinner I had in my life!

What did the interviewer hear in this story? A long list of Brenda's private sensations: I felt, I tasted, I saw, I enjoyed. I was lucky. And it was all true, but what could an interviewer say except "How nice for you"? Of course, sometimes we all just want to talk about treats we enjoyed and feelings we felt. That's not a crime, but when the focus is totally limited to your own inner sensations, and little is done to connect the listener to the experience, it tends to leave that person out. Brenda especially blows it here by beginning with what was relatively frivolous about the experience. She just wallows around in her own sensual pleasure. There's nothing wrong with that when chatting with friends or striking up a conversation on an airplane with a stranger, but this is not how you start an interview. A better approach would have been to focus on what she learned about the people on that island, or to bring up an interesting book she read on the beach. In Appendix B: "Preparing for the Interview," I stress the importance of what you say first.

What could Brenda have said differently? She could have talked about something in her experience that surprised or moved her, something that was not completely focused on herself. When I asked her to do that, she told me that when she first saw the color of the water by the Caribbean shore, that bright turquoise, she almost couldn't believe it.

It wasn't just *sort of* turquoise, the way people will say a cat has "red fur" when it's really just reddish-brown. The water *really was* turquoise, just like the stone, and I hadn't realized water could look that way. I couldn't get over it. I guess it was

---

DANGER SIGN: *"I, I, I, I . . ."*

Listen for the sound of the letter *I*. If, like Brenda, you're hearing it a lot in your own voice, it could be a sign that you're stuck on one topic, a topic that is not automatically interesting for others the way it is for you. This goes for essays as well as interviews. A medical school application essay reader once told me that he *eliminates* any candidate who has ten or more I's, me's, or my's in one essay. I think that's over the top, but in all those I's, he sees red flags that signal unacceptable selfishness.

---

because it was so different, and that made me realize that this wasn't just another beach, this was a whole different place, a different part of the world, where things could be different from what I knew. It made me want to keep my eyes open.

When you go beyond listing sensations and describe something that felt new or important to you, then you begin to give your listener a sense of what you care about and what you stand for. Then you're showing something about your character.

What Brenda told me about the turquoise water showed me that she could look carefully at the world around her and think about what she saw. Her curiosity drew her out of herself and helped her engage with the world, and I knew that colleges would like to see this side of her, all fired up with unselfish curiosity.

Can you do that every time? No. No one can. Some experiences are just sensory pleasures: I ate a candy bar. Yum! The end. But if you can't say more than that, keep the story short. If you find yourself in Brenda's situation, telling an interviewer something purely personal that doesn't feel important to you, then change the subject to something you want the interviewer to know. In the following chapters, we'll cover more about the sides of you that interviewers hope to discover.

YOUR BEST SELF CONNECTS
WITH OTHERS

The mistake all three of these applicants made was falling so deeply into "being themselves" that they seemed to forget anyone else was in the room. Whether it was Stephen announcing his conventional desire for success, or Dave telling jokes his audience couldn't appreciate, or Brenda listing private enjoyments that left the interviewer out, none of them offered an admissions person a reason to listen. You've probably been in class with a poor teacher who loses his students entirely because they can't relate to what he is saying. When it comes to your application, you're the "teacher," and the admissions people are your "students," hoping for some way to connect.

What happens if they don't make that connection? Exactly what happens to you with a teacher who doesn't help you relate. The admissions people get bored. Maybe they're too professional to yawn or fidget, but they still get distracted. They may miss whatever you say next, even if it's good stuff. They may feel resentful and judge you less favorably. They may even make judgments about your character overall, which can give a negative cast to everything they learn about you. "Just being yourself," then, risks making you look plain selfish. To overcome that selfishness, you need to strike a balance between saying what you want to say and helping your listener make a connection.

CAN YOU REALLY DO BOTH?

Hold on a minute. Aren't being yourself and being unselfish really opposites? "When I'm being really myself," one astute counselee told me, "I'm not worrying about what other people think or feel; I'm putting myself first. How am I supposed to balance both at once?"

REVISING THE RULE

~~Just be yourself.~~
Show them your best self.
How? By going beyond the selfish
to connect with others.

My answer: You're exactly right. They *are* opposites. If you try to do both at once, you can easily get frustrated and stuck. When writing an essay, that could mean writer's block. In an interview, that could mean stumbling over your words or making outbursts you regret. The trick is to recognize that "being true to yourself" and "being unselfish" are two different goals, and you should work on them one at a time.

When you're learning to juggle, you start by tossing one ball in the air and catching it with the same hand. It looks kind of strange, but it's the best way to learn to handle the ball. When you can toss the ball so it falls right back to where it started, you're ready to try tossing two balls with one hand. Only then do you work up to three balls with two hands—real juggling. In the same way, finding that balance between being yourself and being unselfish is a juggling act. I suggest you *start* by being focused on yourself, but only for practice, before you work up to unselfishly helping your listener make a connection.

In one instance I remember, a student chose to be selfish in order to work toward her goal of becoming a physician. Mary Beth was a premed student in college. In order to succeed, she saw significantly little of her classmates, and her long hours in summer research labs took her away from time with her family. Her academic commitments caused her to miss all of the bridal parties before her older sister's wedding, and she barely fulfilled her role as

STEPS TO SUCCESS

Whatever aspect of the application you're working on, you'll need to divide your time to allow for three steps:

1. Free expression: "singing" whatever songs you want to sing, to discover which ones express you best
2. Learning what your audience cares about
3. Picking the material that lets you be true to yourself *and* at the same time interest your audience

bridesmaid in the ceremony. One uncle called her "totally selfish," but Mary Beth stuck to her guns and put her research lab commitment first. Later that fall, Mary Beth told her college advisor about her uncle's comment, to which the advisor responded, "Ironically, to get into a selfless profession like medicine, you sometimes have to be selfish."

Sometimes it is justifiable to be selfish, but as seen in Brenda's case, it's never justifiable in an interview. In that one-on-one situation, you have to seek balance between presenting your most genuine self and showing genuine interest in your interviewer and the college.

This is what I do in my practice sessions with applicants, and above, I described my three-step process for managing the stress of preparing your application; this same process will help you manage the tension between being yourself and unselfishly connecting with your admissions people. For now, I'm going to focus on the error of selfishness as it shows up in the different parts of the application. You can find more on interviewing and essay-writing in the step-by-step guides at the end of this book.

UNMAKING THE MISTAKE:
BALANCING YOUR DIFFERENT SELVES

Your Best Self in the Transcript
and "Brag Sheet"

Your school record and your list of extracurriculars and special achievements (the "brag sheet") is a record of the choices you've made over four years. It shows how you balanced being yourself— following your own personal interests and choosing how much challenge to take on—with shaping yourself as an applicant who would appeal to an admissions committee. If you've taken multiple courses in a certain subject area, or if you've stuck with an extracurricular activity for years, both indicate "hot spots" of sustained interest that will set you apart from other candidates. When you avoid challenging courses such as advanced placement classes, especially in subject areas in which you say you are highly interested, you suggest you prefer staying comfortable to exerting yourself in the subjects that supposedly fascinate you. In this way, your record begins to tell a story about you. This story involves showing (or hiding) your passions, which I cover in depth in Chapter Four, "Nothing Turns You On."

Your Best Self in Recommendation Letters

Admissions committees always want to know "Does this applicant participate in class?" Class participation is considered so important because it shows a mix of knowledge, enthusiasm, and willingness to go beyond selfishness and help everyone learn together. It's a mix that professors crave, and admissions people always look for it in recommendation letters. But not all class

participation is positive. Sometimes selfishness turns class participation into a negative:

- Some students speak up a lot but in ways that seem only
  attention-grabbing or immature. Their remarks can lead frustrated teachers to make small, highly damaging remarks in
  recommendation letters, such as "John speaks up in class with
  jokes and asides but contributes less when the discussion turns
  serious." Or even worse: "Judy enjoys the sound of her own
  voice, and we hear from her on every subject."

- Other students, especially those who are persuasive and articu-
  late, use their gifts to take control of the class. Some feel they
  must respond to every other student's remarks, competing
  with the teacher to be the one in charge.

- I knew one very smart kid who bragged about his ability to get
  the math teacher off topic by the end of every class. It turned
  out that the math teacher figured out what he was doing and
  made a point of describing it to the guidance counselor, who
  mentioned it in his recommendation letter.

No matter where you are in your high school career, there is still time
to change the impression you're making on teachers with your style
of class participation. Ask yourself: Am I showing my best self when
I speak up in class? Am I talking just for me, or to connect with the
teacher and the other students? If you're not sure, you might talk to
your teachers or ask a fellow student how you sound.

Does this amount to extra work? Well, it does. And I realize that
not every class may inspire you to such efforts. But remember, it's not
about a single class. You're auditioning for college. So for now, you
can start by phasing out your classroom comments that could seem
selfish or immature. In later chapters, we'll consider the kinds of
comments that are most helpful.

Your Best Self in Interviews

In a practice interview, Donna started to talk about the summer she spent in Vermont:

> Almost every night I saw the sunset, and it made me think about nature's beauty. A lot of my friends are environmentalists. They say I don't think enough about all the threats it faces. But being out-of-doors makes me realize how lucky I am to go to Vermont in the summers. And it's exciting to have a job outside, keeping hiking trails clean in these mountains every day. There was really a lot of garbage sometimes that we had to clean up. I was surprised. I'd come over a hill and there would be this garbage and I would think, I could see *that* in the city. And I like the energy of a city, but I learn more about myself in the hills.

One observer commented later: "She seemed to have a nice summer, but she didn't say anything."

Don't be what I call a conversational "skimmer," zipping from one thought to another without ever going below the surface. Skimming suggests that you don't seem to care strongly about what you're saying, or whether your listener is interested.

To help Donna go deeper, I asked, "Why did you want to talk about this? What makes the wilderness interesting to you?"

"I don't know," she answered. "I didn't really think about that."

It's worth thinking about. If you're not interested in what you're saying, if you don't care, chances are your listeners won't learn what you care about. As I've said, this kind of talk can seem selfish—it gives the impression that you've forgotten there is another person there listening to you, and it sounds like you're just thinking to yourself out loud to pass the time.

In my follow-up conversation with Donna, I asked, "Did you learn anything about yourself in Vermont?"

"I guess," she said. "But I wouldn't know how to explain it."

"Well," I said, "did anything surprise you, in terms of your feelings or reactions while you were there?"

She didn't respond right away. I was glad, because a pause to think is usually a sign of something brewing. After a minute she said, "The littering made me angry. When I saw it on the trails, I'd really get mad. Usually I'm not very political, but the way people treated that beautiful place made me wish I could do something."

With that comment, she began to discover one of the reasons she cared about her summer. She'd discovered a genuine personal interest that was also something a listener could understand. And at that moment, without any tricks or artificial coaching, I observed a change in her manner. She spoke with more focus and energy. She made eye contact. The conversation started to take us somewhere, together.

In Appendix B I describe my method for practice interviews, but before you try anything that formal, you'd do well to spend some stress-free time "browsing" through your everyday conversations to notice topics that you tend to find interesting. Remember, although being yourself on its own isn't enough, it *is* step one. So pay attention when you hear yourself saying what you feel like saying. Discover where it leads. If you notice yourself getting fired up about certain topics, you might want to start a list of those topics. Ask yourself: Why do I care about this so much? You may not have an answer yet, but asking the question will start you on your way. When you begin practice interviews, you'll have some interesting material to draw on.

One student who had suddenly become interested in participating in improvisation spoke in his practice interview with us with great enthusiasm: "When I first saw it onstage in our school, it was amazing to me. I knew that was for me." But when we asked, he couldn't say why it was amazing to him and why it was for him. He was a bright kid; he could say why by the time of his first real interviews, but this is an example of why it's critical to practice.

Your Best Self in the Essay

For essays, showing your best self starts the same way as for interviews: You need to interest both yourself and your reader. But when you're writing, you don't have the reader sitting across from you, showing with his or her reactions whether you're getting through. For this reason, it's a good idea to make sure that the subject you're writing about is not just personal, but universal. *Universal* doesn't mean "very very big" and "important," it means that anyone—anyone in the universe, I suppose—can connect with it. It's universal the way type O blood is the "universal donor": Anyone can receive it.

How do you know if you have a universal topic? Here's an example of an essay about an autobiographical writing class, by a senior named Heather. Does it seem to you to get beyond the writer's personal story?

Throughout the term, and especially at the beginning, I spent a lot of time reviewing my term papers with Mr. Stash. My first paper focused on my earlier childhood, when

---

DANGER SIGN: *Rehearsed speeches*

Why *not just memorize answers to interview questions?*

I've said that an application is an audition, but while it's great to prepare topics that you and your interviewer can both enjoy, it's not helpful to prepare precise interview responses in advance, the way you might prepare a song phrase by phrase for an audition. If you sound like you're reciting a prepared answer, your interviewer will feel pushed away, as if you're taking the stage and sending the interviewer to find a seat in the audience. The goal of interview preparation is to get comfortable having a spontaneous conversation about topics that matter to you. It's not to give a speech.

my family moved from southern California to Philadelphia. In this paper I got to see the major aspects of my life when I came to the East Coast. While writing it I remembered with some nostalgia my memories from middle school. My next written assignment for him was about the camp I had been going to every summer for all of my life; in many ways it felt like my real home because my family has moved so often. The first draft was slightly confused, because I had so many fond memories I wanted to include, but Mr. Stash helped me to extensively edit the essay, and sift out the most important aspects of that camp experience. From his suggestions I was able to write a paper that showed me why I really loved the place. Once again, writing the paper brought back a rush of memories, and as Mr. Stash helped me to give these memories more meaning I learned a great deal about myself.

So far, I was bored to death, and I hadn't learned much about Heather I could relate to. She reviews some memories of childhood, and the teacher who helped her "learn about herself." The essay might work as an English paper in a personal writing class, because it does have a thesis, a main point: *Writing with Mr. Stash taught me about myself.* But if you're not the writer or the teacher who assigned it, who cares? The essay was only about her own vague sentimental feelings.

I told Heather I found it hard to relate to her story, and suggested that in order to move from the personal to the universal, she could try making a list of the universal topics or subjects she had mentioned in her draft, aside from her personal experience. She came up with these:

1. Writing classes
2. Working closely with a teacher
3. Memories
4. Living in different places, not having a home

These are topics that might interest anyone—we've all had homes, memories, teachers, and classes. Anyone might be interested to learn something about them, since anyone can relate. I asked her, "What do you think your essay says about any one of these universal topics?"

"I'm not sure what you mean," she said.

"Take memories," I told her. "The personal story is that Mr. Stash helped you bring up memories, and you discovered something in them. And it could happen to anyone, so that's a universal topic: *Mr. Stash helped me discover how memories reveal their meaning when you write about them.* Is that what interested you about this experience?"

"Not really," she said.

"Okay," I said.

After a pause, she said, "I guess the thing is that my family moved so often, and I felt like I didn't really have a home. But I had camp. I didn't realize it for a while, because I didn't live there, but when I wrote about it, that was what felt like home. That was my home. A home doesn't have to be the place you wake up every day. I think that's what I really want to say: that I learned something I didn't know before, about what makes a home a home."

With that, Heather moved from a purely personal story—"I learned about myself"—to a universal one: "Let me tell you what for me makes a home a home."

Now consider a different essay, with a different kind of challenge. George, who had never gotten very excited about history or social studies, came alive in those classes when he became fascinated by the Austro-Hungarian Empire. His teacher, without consulting George's guidance counselor, was thrilled with George's newfound enthusiasm, and encouraged him to write his personal statement about these tyrants and the ingenious ways they controlled their people.

George wrote an essay with a good universal point: "I am impressed by these great leaders' achievements, militarily, economically, and especially in terms of their sheer power over their people." In his essay, his enthusiasm and fascination came through, but the trouble was that he seemed too emotionally involved with the regime and its dictatorial ways, which in some aspects anticipated Hitler. Reading his draft, I half expected him to shave his head and join the Neo-Nazi Party. While Heather's initial essay had seemed selfish because it had no universal idea to interest a reader, George's essay had a universal idea, but a scary one. It seemed to show off a side of him that was aggressive and controlling, maybe even threatening.

At our next meeting, I asked about his feelings about democracy and tyranny. I encouraged him to explain both in the essay. He added to the essay and showed the revision to his young history teacher, who objected to the change. He thought his student was not being true to what had motivated his newfound success in social studies: his enthusiasm for the tyrannical regime. This inexperienced teacher also worried that George's enthusiasm would cool if he didn't stay focused on his favorite tyrants. According to this teacher's reasoning, being true to his "authentic energy" was the most important issue, and since George had mentioned in his application that he was Jewish, "he wasn't really going to offend anyone." The teacher felt that George should go back to his first version.

I disagreed. The enthusiasm in his first essay could easily have sounded like approval, and if this essay was someone's one brief chance to get to know him, he could seem like a scary kid to have on campus. Of course, I couldn't rewrite the essay for him. So instead, I described for him the impression that his first version gave me. I explained how it made him sound selfish, because he only seemed to care about what was exciting to him and not whether the ideas could be offensive or even harmful to his reader. Was that the sort of impression he wanted to convey?

He said, "No! This stuff is all really *interesting*, but that doesn't mean I think it's *right*." In his history paper and early drafts of his essay, George had talked only about his fascination, but not about his own values. In his revised essay, he included his appreciation for democracy and egalitarianism in the United States, while discussing how he was fascinated by what happens when too much power is concentrated in the hands of too few—and how dangerous it is to give absolute power to any one person. For me, working with George was a lesson about how easy it is to forget the sensibilities of your readers, and on top of that, your own highest ideals. In the end, his essay made clear his appreciation for democracy and egalitarianism.

Watching the development of George's essay through a few drafts taught me a lot about the slow process of discovering your "best self" in an essay. Your readers need to learn not just about your topic but about your overall attitudes and ideals. This is why I encourage you to alternate between focusing on what interests you and considering your audience as you write your essay. Often, you will come to something even more true to yourself than you would get by just writing your private thoughts. And when your best self emerges, you and your reader can recognize it.

Dangerous Topics: Childhood

In general, if a topic is very interesting to you, then with some work you'll be able to find the universal topic in it. For Heather, what started as a purely private experience opened out into a universal topic—family and home. In George's case, a topic that ran the risk of seeming naïve and selfish (or worse) was redeemed with a more mature perspective. Over the years, though, I've seen that some topics are more trouble than they're worth. They tend to drag writers down with them, into depths of immaturity that admissions people can't relate to. For this reason, I discourage most essays about childhood.

Even if you have an interesting story to tell, when you describe the world as you knew it when you were six or seven or eight years old, you can easily slip into thinking on the level of a six- or seven- or eight-year-old. This can be especially tempting if applying to colleges has left you feeling that the world is too big, too complicated. It can be comforting to write about simpler times, and it may even be therapeutic, but I encourage you to keep those essays for personal use. The thoughts you express in a college essay should be as mature as possible. I have seen that a year or even six months can make a difference in the level of a writer's thinking.

Here are some childhood topics I suggest you avoid:

- Big brother/big sister stories
- Tales of babysitting
- Favorite childhood pet/game/hiding place
- A former home or school and why you miss it
- Childhood basis of a career plan: "I've wanted to a be a doctor since my mom took me to the hospital when I was six. . . ."

Why is childhood a dangerous topic? Because in most instances, you'll be recalling outdated interests, from a time when you weren't very good at connecting with adults. The immaturity and lack of perspective of that time can overshadow the more sophisticated perspective you have today. You may wind up not only writing about childhood but sounding like a child. Of course, there are exceptions. For example, a student who has studied child psychology and development might be able to bring an adult perspective to bear on childhood memories. Or if a student has worked with an abused or economically deprived child and tried to help him, then the personal childhood story might open into a universal social issue. But, in general, when your essay merely describes childhood memories or relationships with younger children, you might miss the chance to move from the "just being yourself" stage of self-expression to a stage that shows your best, most mature thought.

"Just being yourself" can be college application suicide, unless you make it the first step in a longer journey of self-discovery. In later chapters, we'll focus on how to present the sides of yourself that the colleges most want to see. For now, practice what you think is your best self—in person and on paper—and observe the results. Keep thinking about what you like best in yourself and work on showing this to people. And then work on articulating what you've decided about your own values. No one can always be the person she wants to be, but you should at least give a sense of the person you strive to be.

CHAPTER THREE

FATAL MISTAKE #3

Nothing Turns You On

Beware this error if . . .

—*You don't like much about school, or at least you
wouldn't admit that you do*

—*You consider yourself a well-rounded student*

What is the most essential sign of good character in the eyes of admissions committees? What one thing, when it's missing, marks you as simply not college material? There is one quality that admissions people believe has an almost magical power to create successful college experiences. This quality is intellectual passion. Everyone has this quality, but not everyone knows how to tap into it or how to show an admissions committee that it's there.

In the *Star Wars* universe, there is one test that sets good apart from evil: whether you rely on "the Force" or "the Dark Side" for your power. Admissions people often seem to believe that intellectual passion is a power almost as strong as the Force. If this "force" is within you, they trust you will succeed in college without doing harm either to your fellow students or to the school's reputation. Applicants who display intellectual passion get chosen over others who look better on paper. Those who seem to lack it are as good as dead.

Now, you may be thinking: This is crazy! The Force is intellectual passion?! What does *intellectual passion* even mean? *Intellectual* just means thinking, using your mind. *Passion* suggests enthusiasm, desire, love, and excitement. Put together, *intellectual passion* means the love of learning, a deep excitement for developing and using your mind.

Now, I'm sure that in less than a second you can think of some learning you've done that you definitely *didn't* love. You know very well that high school is not one long passionate encounter of questing minds. Admissions people know that too. But just as a doctor heals the sick and a salesperson sells a product, an admissions officer assembles a community of interested, motivated students in the classroom. That's his or her job. Students who love to learn do the best work and have the most fun doing it, and when word gets out that a college is full of students having a great time doing great work, that college becomes even more desirable. On the other hand, it's hard for admissions people to get excited about students who don't seem to get turned on by anything academic. So, intellectually speaking, you have to show them that *something* turns you on.

How much of a difference does this really make? Once, when I worked as a college counselor in a private high school, I sat in on a meeting with members of the admissions committee of one of the hottest colleges at that time. "Listen to this!" said one of the admissions people. The whole table turned to him as he read aloud from my student's application. "Your school impressed me the most, not just because of your excellent reputation but because your students are well-balanced. They don't study all of the time. They know how to have fun!"

This applicant was not incorrect about the college. The students there, from what I knew of them, did seem to have a good sense of fun. But this correct factual observation about the student body was completely overshadowed for the admissions committee by what the student seemed to be revealing about himself. "I guess he doesn't consider academics fun," said another committee member. They moved his application to the "no" pile.

Why is it lethal if you appear to have only a modest love of learning? Because intellectual passion is one of the few things that colleges can be sure will last through your college career. Your interests may change, your major may change; your whole life may take a direction you didn't plan for at seventeen. Many people's lives do. Music majors wind up studying child psychology or math, poets go to medical school or start up businesses, doctors and lawyers quit to write novels. But if you love to learn, you will bring that passion with you, and it will give you energy and focus for whatever you do in college.

So you need to show colleges your intellectual passions.

WHAT IF I'M NOT SURE?

One of my most academically outstanding students wrote this in his personal essay: "I like all of my subjects fairly well, but I'm still searching for something in school that really turns me on. I haven't found it yet, and maybe I won't find it until I'm in college, or beyond. But I know it's out there." He was trying to say that he hadn't found the area or profession that would hold his interest for the rest of his life. But he *came across as saying* that nothing in his present courses was all that great. How long do you think he lasted in the competition for the top schools? His impressive grades couldn't make up for his lack of genuine passion. He was bright and capable, but he was missing the interest, energy, enthusiasm, and optimism that educators look for.

Admitting uncertainty about what he wanted to pursue in the future was not his mistake. Colleges can live with that kind of uncertainty, and in some ways, they prefer it, because it shows that you're committed to following your intellectual passions wherever they may lead. But colleges are wary of any student who seems to lack intellectual passion in the present.

WHAT IF I DON'T LOVE ANYTHING?

Many students tell me, especially if we've only just met, that they have no passions, at least not for school. Maybe you feel that way too. Maybe you think you're just not that kind of person.

If you feel like you're the applicant without intellectual passion, or without enough to get excited about, try this. Consider the history classes and the English classes you've taken. Which have you preferred? I find that most students have a clear preference, but they may not realize the reason. Literature mostly concentrates on individuals, their private feelings and thoughts in relation to others and to society. History, in contrast, focuses on the public goals of leaders and the values of societies themselves. Your preference for one or the other suggests you have more of an interest either for understanding the situation of the individual or for the development of society. That gives you a starting point. Now let's get a little more detailed. Try this:

1. Make a list of all the subjects you've studied.

2. Put a number next to each one, ranking them in order from worst to best. Or, if necessary, rank them instead from truly awful (1, 2, 3) up through semiawful (4, 5, 6) and so on to only partly awful. Now, starting with the relatively nonhorrifying subjects, write down one thing you enjoyed about each, or if nothing comes to mind, write down something that wasn't so bad. If thinking about academic subjects themselves doesn't inspire you, try thinking about different kinds of classroom activities you might have enjoyed doing, even if the official subject didn't excite you. You might have liked classes that involved:

Drawing or drafting
Working with computers

Word puzzles

Reading

Debating

Art activities

Live or video performance

Storytelling

Logic problems

Acting

Dance

Even if you tend to dislike academics, I hope these exercises will bring up some examples of what you do like. If you're the kind of student who does like academics, I hope this is reminding you of some great times you've had in a classroom. The purpose of this exercise is to give you a more detailed list of your own *preferences*. Even if you still can't say that you love any of your subjects, you're prepared now with a list of *what you prefer* that you can talk about in your interviews. If an interviewer asks about your favorite subjects, you can offer honestly, "I prefer [whatever ranked highest]." To answer the follow-up question, "What exactly do you like about that subject?" you can describe a time when the teacher asked you to do something you enjoyed. Now you have some specifics to talk about.

DOESN'T THIS GET EMBARRASSING?

Many students I've worked with discover that when they stop to think about it, there are subjects they enjoy, but they feel awkward talking about them. At many schools, it is not "cool" to get too excited about classes and teachers. An understated style becomes a requirement. And so very often I get reports of interview conversations that go like this one:

INTERVIEWER: So, what subjects do you like best?

APPLICANT: I guess I don't mind math so much. The sciences are a little boring. But psychology is okay.

If you had a high school understatement decoder, you would know that this message is in secret code. It actually means "I like math, but I *love* psychology." However, this applicant was so much in the habit of talking about academics in this flattened-out, "cool" way that she didn't realize she wasn't communicating what she felt. And the interviewer didn't have a decoder. "She thinks everything is so-so!" was the interviewer's impression. The school where she gave this interview was supposed to be the applicant's backup or "safety" school, the relatively less competitive college on her list where she felt sure she would be accepted. After this interview, though, we had to get her a new safety.

AREN'T YOU SUPPOSED TO LOOK "WELL-ROUNDED"?

Many applicants and their parents and advisors have heard that colleges want academically "well-rounded" students. A little science, a little English, a little sports, a little arts—isn't that right? In fact, it's wrong and it's dangerous, because showing a school that you have many small enthusiasms and minor accomplishments suggests that you have only small passions. This may not keep you out of the less competitive colleges, but at higher levels it could be the end of your application.

One of my counselees flooded his colleges with evidence of more activities than he could possibly have participated in seriously. For the fall term of his senior year he listed these weekly commitments:

Varsity soccer—10 hours

Newspaper—3 hours

Student government—2 hours

Community service—2 hours

Tour guide—2 hours

Yearbook—2 hours

Chess club—2 hours

French club—1 hour

Debating society—2 hours

Social planning committee—1 hour

Campaigning for state senator—2–3 hours

Religious youth group—1 hour

Job in pharmacy—4 hours

He didn't seem "well-rounded." He seemed instead like someone with a habit of dabbling in everything without contributing significantly. His applications were widely rejected. Fewer, select commitments are better, and those that are emphasized should show passion and real

REVISING THE RULE

~~Show schools you're well-rounded.~~
Show schools the areas where you feel
the most passion.

contribution. These activities, where a student is "hot," where he or she takes the time to develop ability and talent, are what counts.

SHARE YOUR ENTHUSIASM

Remember the understated applicant, the one who said math isn't that bad, and psychology is okay? Her trouble was that she couldn't communicate her real enthusiasm. Does that mean she should have been a better actor and practiced sounding more enthusiastic than she felt? No. Not only is that dishonest, it's very risky. Interviewers speak to dozens or hundreds of students each year. They have a pretty good eye for authenticity. And beyond that, they have intellectual passion themselves. They know it when they see it, and they don't appreciate seeing it faked.

The trick is to connect with feelings you have but may not recognize or feel comfortable describing to a stranger. In practice interviews, I give students the time to discover which subjects engage them most. I tell them what I've just told you, that an interest is just a preference—I like A better than B—and any preference is positive and worth talking about. As I described in Chapter Two, we give students time just to "be themselves" and to discover whatever academic areas they prefer talking about. And once they get comfortable, something very interesting happens: The understatement and the high school "cool" tends to melt away on its own, and it becomes easier for them to talk about things they actually like. And then something like this can happen— Denise was talking to me about her "preferences" exercise:

"It kind of took me by surprise," she said. "I was all okay with your rule: Don't start with the ones I *don't* like. I put those away. Then the ones that sometimes get on my nerves, like the sciences; I didn't put them down either. Okay. And what was left that I liked? English, of course, and theater, so that's where I started. And then number three, calculus, which was required for us, but there it was. I'm a poetry person, and before I had to take calculus, I really never thought I cared about math. But once I learned the symbols you work with and I realized I could do it, I could find the right answers, it was fascinating!"

She lit up as she talked about it. It wasn't just what she said, it was how she said it. And when she said it for real to her interviewers, one of them told me, "She got me to listen." Had she begun with the courses she liked the least, she might have lost the interviewers' interest before she got to what turned her on. Admissions people are on the lookout for intellectual passion not just in the words a student uses, but in the way the student's attitude changes as he or she speaks. "I look for the energy and sparkle in the eyes," said one of Middlebury's admissions officers. Of course, energy alone won't do it. Neither will statements of fact: I love this, I love that. It's the combination of the sparkle and the substance, the evidence that a particular student is speaking from both the head and the heart, that signals intellectual passion.

When you talk about things you like, you'll find that the interview feels more interesting, not just for you, but for the interviewer. When you feel interested, you build up more enthusiasm and speak with feeling about subjects you care for—and then you've done it! You've shared some of your intellectual passions with the interviewer.

(Don't worry. Your friends don't have to know unless you want to tell them.)

SHARE YOUR SPECIAL EXPERTISE

Chris told his interviewer, "I love to talk politics. I can think about that stuff all day. Especially social issues, the real hot-button issues, conservative versus liberal. That stuff's great."

"So I suppose you read a good deal about those issues?"

"I guess," Chris said.

The interviewer named a recent political best-seller and asked if Chris had read it.

"No," Chris said. "I take my schoolwork pretty seriously, so I don't have time for a lot of outside reading."

This was a mistake. Chris did not need to have read that particular book, but admissions people expect that a passionate interest will inspire outside learning, and especially outside reading. If you love literature, they expect you'll find time to read novels on your own. If you're interested in engineering, they'll expect that you've read some journals. NASCAR fans read the sports page; dog breeders read specialty dog magazines. An interest isn't an interest if you don't want to learn more about it. So if you haven't read and learned about your interests outside of school, you'll sound like a phony, or a nonreader.

What could Chris have done? Besides getting to know the hot political book titles, he could have recognized that admissions people are not just looking for a list of books, they're looking for signs of passionate learning. Chris didn't read a lot of books, but he did read political blogs like the Drudge Report, and he listened to political talk radio. He could have explained how fascinating it was that people from different backgrounds saw the most compelling political issues differently. In other words, he did have a passionate interest in American politics and social issues, and he was doing a kind of "field research" on his own every day. He had the knowledge, but he didn't recognize that his kind of reading and learning "counts." This is what I think of as "special expertise." Through listening he had developed a kind of knowledge and perspective that was as valuable as formal study.

In a practice session, I asked him, "Why don't you read more books about politics?"

"What I think is really cool," he said, "is not the experts with their canned opinions. I like to hear what regular people are thinking about, all kinds of people. Because the experts are often just pushing their own point of view, when what I like is to know how people make up their own minds. I find that in newspaper editorial pages, where people write in their reactions to articles written by the editors."

With this answer, Chris began to show that his intellectual passion had given rise to an area of special expertise, based on his own private research. That was even more impressive than having read the

STEPS TO SUCCESS

B e ready to talk about your private reading, whether in an interview, an essay, or even in class.

1. Most interviewees can come up with a title or two they've read, but do yourself a favor and review your reading for the last year, so you can be selective about what you'd most like to talk about.

2. Be ready to talk about specific books you've enjoyed. If you read magazines or journals, know their names too. Most impressive is to know the names of the writers. Why? Because it shows that you're interested in the thinking of the writer.

latest political best-seller. With this perspective, Chris became much more effective in interviews.

Lawrence loved to play the jazz guitar. For the last couple of years, he'd played a little rock and folk, popular songs like those his friends played. Then one day he heard his teacher playing old Django Reinhardt records and he flipped. Now Lawrence loved Django and was playing his recordings whenever he got the chance, two or three hours a day. Even playing scales felt good to him. So when he was asked in an interview about his interests, he mentioned jazz.

"Ah," said his interviewer, "I guess you listen to MJQ?"

"MJQ?"

"Modern Jazz Quartet?"

Lawrence wasn't even sure if that was an album or a group. He froze.

What do you do if you're asked about a book or some other reference you've never even heard of? Remember that the point is not to seem like an expert. The point is to show your intellectual passion. And if you have the passion, then whatever you don't know yet, you can learn. "There's so much great jazz out there," Lawrence said in response. "Is MJQ one of your favorites?" The interviewer was proba-

INTERVIEW FIRST AID

I f you're asked about a book or a subject you're not familiar with, don't panic. Instead, show an interest in what the interviewer is saying. You can ask, "What was important to you about it?" A response like this shows the interviewer that you regard any situation, even a college interview, as a chance to learn and to grow intellectually. That's more impressive than identifying titles or authors on demand.

bly flattered that Lawrence was interested in his opinion. He told Lawrence what he loved about MJQ, and Lawrence talked about Django Reinhardt. At the end of the interview, they wrote down recommendations for each other. Lawrence had shown that although he was a young jazz fan, he was a sincere one.

SHOW YOUR OPEN, CURIOUS MIND

Students with passionate interests often hold strong views. They have perceptions about the things that interest them, and they've thought about them enough to express opinions. One counselee of mine had strong feelings on the issue of abortion and wrote the following:

> There are no circumstances that warrant the killing of a baby
> at any stage of development, no matter what the excuse. It is
> just plain murder. It amazes me that anyone can even speak
> up for the side of murder.

When I recommended that she choose another essay topic, she thought I was saying that her views were wrong. I told her that on their campuses, colleges like to have conservatives and liberals and everything in between. However, this essay introduction didn't just show an opinion. It showed a lack of interest in the views of the other side.

Colleges seek thinkers who can see more than one side of an issue and are open to the possibility of learning something new. If you portray yourself as completely closed to arguments besides the one you believe, you show political passion, but not intellectual passion. You sound like you don't want to learn. And, as I've said, if you don't have intellectual passion, you're as good as dead.

LINK YOUR HEART AND MIND IN THE APPLICATION

Your course list and your extracurriculars show a lot about you, including what you care about enough to choose when you have a choice. Suppose you love the space program and everything having to do with NASA. An admissions person might ask questions like these while looking over your application: Did you love it enough to join the science club? Did you love it enough to participate in a science fair? Were you excited enough by astrophysics to take AP physics and AP chemistry? In these ways, your transcript and "brag sheet" can help identify your "hot spots," confirming the strength of your intellectual passions and your willingness to do some work to nourish them.

Admissions people will expect to see that you brought your passions with you to school, that you talked about them in class or with teachers, that you are known for the things you care about, and that those things are mentioned in your recommendation letter from a teacher or guidance counselor. And, remember, it's never too late to share these interests with your teachers and guidance counselors.

LINK YOUR HEART AND MIND IN THE INTERVIEW

Besides asking questions about specific areas that interest you, interviewers will also be looking for signs that you want to grow intellectually, and even that you enjoy the methods of learning. Some interviewers ask, for example, which of your term papers or shorter essays you enjoyed writing the most. They are less interested in creative writing, because creative writing is not a crucial tool in every discipline, but academic essays are required in every department. Now, I've noticed that high school students often treat it as a kind of rule that they hate term papers, hate to have them assigned, hate to write them, hate to talk about them. This isn't everyone, of course, but there seems to be peer pressure to at least say they weren't fun. So what do you do if you're asked this question straight out?

It's best if you can say that you enjoy writing essays, or at least that you're beginning to like them. Consider the essays you've written. Perhaps you enjoyed writing an essay on a topic that especially interested you? If that's not true, you might at least acknowledge that you see why writing essays is important: how writing about a subject makes you look at it more carefully, and see it more deeply than you did before. Ideally, you'd have an example or two, ready to talk about, that shows how your way of thinking was shaped or changed by engaging with a topic in an essay.

What I hope you won't do is use your interview to talk about what you actively dislike about academics. You are entitled to your opinion, of course, but you can be pretty sure that if someone has chosen it as a job to interview college applicants, that person is going to be pretty positive about academics. You're not going to change anyone's mind. (Imagine you had an audience with the pope. Would you argue with him against the existence of God?) So, if you've had boring teachers or pointless classes, or if you don't see why anyone makes teenagers study poetry or trigonometry or foreign languages, remember that to a lover of academics, these complaints may suggest that you find all of education, even all of college, boring and stupid and pointless. Even if you feel that way at times, review Fatal Mistake #1 and use your brief interview time to score some points.

LINK YOUR HEART AND MIND
IN THE ESSAY

There's a simple way to show your intellectual passions in an essay: Write about something you care about. That means that when you choose a subject for your main essay(s), make sure you take the time to give yourself a real choice. By now, perhaps you've already tried out my approach for discovering what you'd like to talk and write about. Once you have found a subject that interests you, the key is to say something about it that is original or at least from your own heart. People who are passionate about a subject don't just familiarize themselves with other people's ideas on it. Over time, they have their own ideas, as well. Now, if you're just starting to work on your essays, this may make you feel worried. What if you don't have any interesting, passionately held ideas you want to write about? The answer is: Don't worry. You're not supposed to have them when you're just starting to work with a topic. The way you arrive at an interesting idea is by taking a subject you care about and reworking it on paper until you find out what you think.

Let me give an example. Laura decided to write about the American war in Iraq. She followed it on television and in news magazines, and she was strongly opposed to it. In this way, the subject had the potential to show off both her passion for the topic and her commitment to educating herself about it on her own. But what more could she say about it? She thought about writing her essay as an argument against the war, but the ideas that came to her were familiar. Antiwar protestors had already articulated her feelings in the media, and she felt—rightly, I'd say—that she shouldn't use up her one chance to write for her admissions committees by repeating familiar arguments.

How to write about it, then? At school, she was sometimes known as "Liberal Laura," which she didn't appreciate. She began her essay this way:

Why are my classmates so invested in this word, "liberal"? Liberal isn't some separate species, or even a specific kind of person. I'm opposed to the war in Iraq, but not because I'm a liberal-type person. I'm opposed to it because I've learned about it, and what I've learned makes me worry about our future. But all I hear at school is this label. Liberal! Liberal!

Laura wasn't happy with her essay. I wasn't either. There didn't seem to be much to say about being labeled as a liberal. As we talked, I asked her why, for her, personally, the war seemed wrong.

"It's not because I'm some sort of flag burner. I think of myself as pretty patriotic, actually. I love this country, and I'm afraid of what this war is doing to it, of how it's changing our values. *I'm afraid my country will lose its goodness.*"

We were both silent for a moment. Who among us would not be touched by that last statement?

"I guess I should put that in the essay," she said.

"Seems like a good idea," I agreed. With those eight words, she discovered her own idea on a subject she was passionate about, and she created a powerful conclusion to her essay.

Another student, Asher, took the other side of the issue. He wrote about why he agreed with the government's reaction after September 11, the decision to respond to an attack with strength. He acknowledged some of the opinions of pessimistic friends, who said America was ruining its international reputation, but he ended with this thought of his own:

> I hate to see my country so angry, and I would like to see it more loved in the world. But based on what I know of human history, especially Jewish history, I know that if you show a violent enemy that you are weak, it can lead to disaster. I want my country to be tough.

These two essays, though they come from opposite political positions, have in common a deep personal interest or concern that gave

STEPS TO SUCCESS

Show schools the intellectual areas where you feel the most passion.

How?
- Share the areas for which you feel your enthusiasm
- Demonstrate your special expertise (with extra reading or active participation)
- Let them see your open, curious mind at work

rise, through rewriting and rethinking, to a striking and original idea. These essays don't just tell colleges that the writers have intellectual passions, they show originality, how those passions led to original thought.

CHAPTER FOUR

FATAL MISTAKE #4

You Don't Understand Leadership

Beware this error if . . .

—*You think your accomplishments will speak for themselves*
—*You tend to be private or shy*

Jane wanted to present herself as a promising social science major. Although she usually got top grades in those classes, she had received a B-minus grade in history. Her plan was to use her interview as a chance to explain the inconsistent grade. It was only partially her fault, she told her first interviewer. "I didn't do well in that class because I could hardly stay awake. The teacher put us all to sleep! He was so uninspired."

Without hesitation, the interviewer responded: "So what did you do to make the class more interesting?"

Jane was shocked by this reply. She couldn't even answer.

What went wrong? Jane wasn't just taken by surprise by the interviewer's strong response. She was left speechless because she didn't understand the character issue the interviewer had raised: Beyond the question of one bad grade or one bad teacher, the interviewer wanted to know if Jane could exercise leadership.

Leadership is one of the most frequently used—and frequently misunderstood—words in the whole college application process. "Leaders," we often hear, are desirable to schools because they "contribute to the community." I agree. After intellectual passion, I think the next most important quality schools look for in applicants is leadership. But what does this really mean? Contribute what? Lead how?

Most applicants equate *leadership* and *contribution* with participation in sports teams, student government, or the arts, and it's true that these areas provide chances to demonstrate leadership. A star sports player can help bring out the best in the whole team, perhaps leading them to a championship. A great theater director can turn a pretty good play into a moving and memorable one. But each school has only a few sports stars, a few leaders of arts activities, a few top editors on the paper, and so on. Are *leadership* and *contribution* just code words for grabbing the spotlight and getting to be in charge?

No. What counts as leadership to colleges is not just being the president or captain or star. Holding a title doesn't in itself contribute to anything more than the length of your brag sheet. When admissions people read that brag sheet, they ask: Well, okay, but what sort of leader was this person? They mean: What sort of impact did you have

REVISING THE RULE

~~Leadership means being in charge, holding positions like president, team captain, director, or star.~~

Leadership means asserting yourself to help others have more success. What leaders contribute leads to a better experience for all.

on your peers in the school community? While some state universities look mainly at titles and grades and test scores, taking a by-the-numbers approach, many public schools and most private schools look for students who not only excel themselves, but also bring out the best in those around them. The team captain who helps the other players keep their focus and commitment through a long, tough season is not just important because she's captain, but because she keeps the whole team going strong. The class president who helps the class reach a community service goal is equally valuable. Positions of authority give you the opportunity to exert leadership, and it's important to show how you made the most of them.

BUT DON'T THEY REALLY WANT HIGH SCORES?

Some applicants find this hard to believe. Why should leadership matter so much to a college? Wouldn't they rather just have the students with the highest test scores and the most impressive grades and qualifications? Some years ago, there was a new dean of admissions at one of the most competitive small colleges in the country. This dean directed the admissions committee to admit the new class based on their paper credentials without regard to intellectual passion or leadership or other aspects of character. The next first-year class was the most impressive ever on paper, but very quickly professors began to complain. Classroom discussions were stumbling and awkward. Student groups were losing membership. It seemed as if the new students spent all their time alone in their rooms, studying, trying to be top of the class—and there weren't enough students left to make a functioning community. Within a couple of years, the admissions director left the college under faculty pressure and the experiment was ended.

ARE THERE MANY CHANCES
TO BE A LEADER?

There are chances to lead not just on the playing field, in the arts, or in student organizations. Colleges are also looking for leaders crucial to life in the classroom and in the dorms.

Leadership in the Classroom

When I was a college counselor at Andover, almost invariably the admissions people asked: "Does this student speak up in class?" I have already discussed the importance of classroom participation in the chapter about intellectual passion, because participation can show that you love to learn and have the curiosity, enthusiasm, and inner commitment that make a successful student. But these same qualities can also benefit the community of students around you.

When you speak in class with energy and enthusiasm, you lend your excitement to the whole class, keeping up morale, restoring flagging interest, and reminding everyone that you think an academic class can be fun. When you ask questions, you help others to check how well they understand the material. When a teacher answers your questions, those answers help fill in the gaps in everyone's knowledge. Your questions also help the teacher gauge how well the class understands the material and adjust his or her speed and approach. You also might inspire other students to open up. For everyone else in the room, it's nice to hear a range of voices, rather than just one or a few over and over again.

When you relate a topic to your own life, or share your own way of getting to a solution, you help others make personal connections to the material as well, helping them to discover the relevance of the class and to understand that there are a variety of ways to approach even technical subjects. Even your personal, outside reading can be an opportunity to provide leadership in the classroom. If you've read other novels by the writer you are studying in a literature class, technical journal articles about a subject in a science class, or articles about the country you're discussing in a class on politics or economics, you can add perspective to a discussion and enrich it for the entire group.

Think over any class you enjoyed. You probably remember certain students from the class who seemed almost as important as the teacher. You may sometimes have come into class wondering what they were going to say. These "unpaid teaching assistants" can make a good teacher's class great, and a weak teacher's class bearable. That's classroom leadership.

Now think back to Jane, whose interviewer wanted to know how she had made a boring class more interesting. What could she have done differently? She could have made herself a force for learning in her classes. How?

By talking to the teacher about her desire to connect more with the class.

By talking to her friends about why they were tuning out, and then thinking of some questions she could ask that would make a bridge from the teacher to the other students.

By recognizing that if the teacher is a weak leader, then that teacher needs help from a strong student leader.

Does that sound like a lot to do? It is. And I'm not saying you have to do all of it, every time. Most students are leaders more in some kinds of classes and less in others. But, bottom line, whom would you rather sit next to in college, someone who complains about a class, or someone who tries to lead the way to something better?

Leadership in the Dorms

Once in a dorm at a school where I worked, a socially awkward boy was picked on and bullied by boys on his floor, who otherwise seemed like decent people. The picked-on student was a little too formal and self-conscious in his manner, and he didn't want to complain to the administration or physically fight back. One night some of the other students wrecked their victim's room. They threw his bedding on the floor; they emptied his drawers and scattered the contents down the hall. Everyone on the hall saw what had happened, but no one spoke up.

Afterward, though, one of the other boys helped his shaken hallmate pick up his clothes and put his room back together, and apologized to him for not having helped him defend himself. Then he took him to a nearby hangout and spent the evening getting to know him as a person. They became friends, and when the other boys on the hall saw this, the hazing stopped. That was quiet but assertive leadership.

Another time, in a football locker room, I heard a player telling his teammates that he had broken up with his girlfriend of two years because he learned that before they'd gotten together, she'd had several escapades with other guys. One of the boys on the team, hearing his teammate pontificating about the "whore" who had "violated his trust completely" said, "And, Tom, how many girlfriends were you with before your relationship with Kathy? Or was she your first?" There was silence for a long, awkward moment and then the other teammates broke in with, "Yeah, Tom. You're a slut, Tom! Who's the whore here anyway? Maybe she should dump you, Tom." And the whole attitude toward Kathy changed, just because one individual was willing to take the risk of challenging a ridiculous but deeply ingrained double standard.

These examples may seem far from conventional measures of leadership, yet these kinds of personal interventions can prevent far more damaging situations from developing, which allows everyone to get on with all the things they came to school to do. High school guidance counselors keep an eye out for this kind of personal leadership, and admissions people know how important it is. Between two roughly equal candidates, admissions people will always strongly prefer the one who seems more likely to be the more honest student, the more supportive roommate, the more compassionate friend, and the more active participant in the life of the college. Wouldn't you?

A SPECIAL CHALLENGE: SHYNESS

Leadership is harder to demonstrate for students who are shy. You may be passionate about a topic, well-read, and eager to work, but if you are unwilling to talk about your passion in public with your classes or with your peers, then from the point of view of the community, you aren't so different from a bored, apathetic student, on the one hand, or a totally selfish student on the other. You don't add to the conversation. I know this may seem unfair, especially because shy students can be some of the hardest-working and most devoted of all. But shyness can keep you from contributing, and not contributing can be a killer.

Henry was a gifted but shy poet who couldn't bring himself to share his poems with anyone beyond a few trusted friends and one supportive English teacher. The teacher wrote in her recommendation letter that his work was "as powerful as that of any student she had taught, full of real promise." Henry's "reach" school was known for its writing department, and his interviewer was able to draw him out to get him talking. The interviewer urged him to send in copies of his poetry as part of his application. Unfortunately, when Henry got home, he decided not to tell anyone about this request. He kept his writing to himself, sharing it neither with the admissions committee nor with his peers, and in the end his dream school turned him down.

For a lot of shy students, the big challenge is classroom participation. The only answer is to find a way to contribute. I've seen various approaches help shy students join the conversation:

If sitting in a group makes it hard to think of questions or comments, then try preparing them the night before class. Go in with notes, so you don't have to gather your thoughts on the fly and in public. I had a shy student once who was frequently embarrassed by his history teacher, who liked to call on quiet students randomly. I encouraged him to prepare two or three pertinent questions for each class and to jump in with his questions before the teacher turned her attention to him. This strategy earned him a full grade improvement in the class.

If even prepared comments are too uncomfortable to present in class, try talking to the teacher before the class and sharing ideas then. Afterward the teacher can tell the other students, "I was talking to one of you in my office, who suggested [such and such an idea]." That's helpful to everyone. You might even motivate other students to make use of the teacher's office hours. All these are welcome contributions.

If in your private reading you come across material that might be relevant to class, or personal artifacts that relate to a time or a place you're studying, you might also bring these to share with the teacher. Again, the result is that you enrich the class and, of course, your teacher knows it.

Consider asking someone to help you to become a little more vocal in class. Ask a good friend who likes to talk in class to sit beside you and respond to your questions or statements, acknowledging their relevance and importance. Or he or she could do it with a nudge if you think that might help. Sometimes it makes a difference to have someone tell you that you did well after you've taken the risk of asserting yourself. Some teachers can be helpful in overcoming classroom shyness. Guidance counselors and therapists may also have useful suggestions. I know that not everyone can become comfortable with classroom discussion, but it's worth trying both for the sake of your community and for yourself.

If you are shy and the topic comes up in an interview, you can strengthen your position if you can say that you understand the importance of having something to contribute, and that you are working toward that goal. If you make it clear that overcoming shyness is not just something your parents or teachers have instructed you to do, but something you would like to do for the sake of your classmates, your interviewer will still know you can be shy, but he or she will also know that you can be generous and mature in the face of a shortcoming.

WHAT SHOULD A SCHOOL DO FOR ME?

In an interview at an exceedingly competitive university, one rather arrogant student of mine said to his interviewer, "My guidance counselor tells me that I have the courses and grades that you like and also the SATs and leadership stuff that you look for. So [with an arrogant smile] what can your college do for *me*?"

The admissions person responded, "Your record does put you in the top five percent of our candidates, but even in that stratosphere, we can only take half. So," he asked with a matching smile, "why should we take you?" Our boy was dumbstruck, and completely fizzled for the very few minutes remaining. His egotism and overconfidence had finished him on the spot.

You may be thinking: Wait a minute. Isn't an interview your

chance to "interview" the school, too? Shouldn't I be finding out what they have to offer? The answer is yes, but that has to come second. This takes us back to the lesson of Fatal Mistake #2: You have to show your best self at all costs. Everyone applies to college hoping to have an enriching and useful experience that will yield benefits for decades to come. Everyone. But you shouldn't be in their face about it, behaving like some scrutinizing, judgmental consumer. It is infinitely better to emphasize that you want to be sure you are a good fit for their great college.

Another student, Hank, applied to the same highly competitive university despite the doubts of his guidance counselor. Hank's grades were slightly under this college's bar, and he never got great scores on standardized tests.

"We're seeing several students from your school this year," the interviewer told Hank, "and frankly your grades aren't tops and you haven't held any notable leadership positions. Why do you think we'll take you?"

"Because I'm interested in what counts!" Hank blurted out. And it was true—he was truly passionate about literature, and could talk about South American novelists or twentieth-century poetry with the energy and enthusiasm most boys reserved for sports. He sang and wrote songs for a punk band, he played classical oboe, and he knew more about the history of San Francisco (where his family had lived in the same house for four generations) than most adults who lived there. He treated his interviewer to one of the most interesting con-

---

UNMAKING THE MISTAKE

~~You go in with the attitude, "What should this college be offering me?"~~

Ask yourself, "What do I have to contribute to this college?"

versations he'd had in a long time, not by listing these interests, but by engaging the interviewer in conversation about them. Hank gave the impression of someone so excited to be surrounded by other smart, motivated college students that he couldn't wait to get started.

So what happened? The university found a spot for him. He seemed to have so much to contribute in so many surprising ways that they couldn't turn him down.

SHOWING WHAT YOU CAN CONTRIBUTE IN THE INTERVIEW

Some interviewers will ask directly: "What do you think you can contribute to this college?" Others will ask open-ended questions and see what you volunteer. Even bland-sounding interview questions like "Are you enjoying your visit?" and "What do you like to do with your free time?" aren't just icebreakers. They are chances for interviewers to see if you cared enough about their community to learn about it in advance, and what you might add to the community if you joined it. Their reasoning is that if you're excited about an interest, you'll be looking for the chance to act on it.

Whether they ask direct questions or open-ended ones, your interviewers will still be looking for evidence that you can picture yourself deeply and happily involved at their school. It's worth taking some time to consider in advance which departments and which on-campus activities stand out for you. I encourage my students to do as many of these before their interviews as they can manage:

Look over the course catalog, so you are prepared to talk about specific departments, and maybe even specific classes, that would be a good match for you.

Walk through the campus to see the announcements from student groups you might like to join, and events you might like to attend. Look at bulletin boards and read campus news-papers.

Talk to current students about what their standout experiences have been, whether in class or out.

If you don't have the chance to visit in person before your inter-view, check the school's online resources. You may be able to ac-cess the course catalog over the Internet, and the admissions office might be able to give you telephone numbers or e-mail ad-dresses of students willing to talk to applicants.

Does this sound like a lot of preparation and commitment for a school that hasn't even accepted you? It does involve some preparation, but it's not real commitment. No one expects you to declare a major or pick courses or sign up for organizations while you're still in high school. But if you show that you care enough to learn about the school in advance, and that you're already excited enough to imagine your-self there, those are signs that you will have a lot to contribute, and that you're motivated to do so.

On the other hand, this is not the time to try to convince the in-terviewer that you are a "real find." Don't try to make a case that you would be a star. If you can show genuine interest and a humble desire to play a part, that's enough.

Another way to demonstrate your intention to contribute is with the questions you ask your interviewer. One of my students asked a great philosophical question in her interview that led to a rich con-versation that contributed to her admission: "What does this univer-sity hope to develop in the character of its students by the time they graduate?" With this question, she showed a mature awareness that every school has a philosophy and a mission, and she suggested that she had the self-awareness to know that she would do best at a school whose philosophy worked with her own goals.

I've heard this question asked in other ways:

"How does this college hope to influence the outlook of its students?"

"Is there a philosophy here that the college hopes will rub off on its student body?"

If you already know about the school's philosophy (often it is spelled out in their literature), you can still ask (with a smile, of course) about how successfully the college's good intentions are rubbing off on its students.

Although questions of this kind can show your serious interest and maturity, you do have to be careful. Interviewers know that it's easy to ask a fancy question but much harder to have a meaningful conversation about it. Chances are, the school's philosophy is one of the reasons the interviewer took his job. He or she may ask you to explain why you approve of the philosophy, or how you would compare it with the approach at other schools to which you're applying. If you express interest, be ready to talk about it for a while.

SHOWING WHAT YOU CAN CONTRIBUTE IN THE ESSAY

While some schools ask specifically for a whole essay about your leadership experience, every school is looking for evidence of it. The essential thing here is not to get distracted by telling your personal story of persistence and triumph. Admissions people read a lot of essays about close ball games and looming newspaper deadlines and struggles of all kinds against difficult odds. They will not be surprised if at the end of your essay you save the day. What they want to see is if you know what leadership means.

My student Albert was an editor of the school newspaper, and he began his essay on an experience as a leader in this way:

DANGER SIGN: *Asking for facts*

I t can be deadly to quiz your interviewers on factual matters. I don't recommend asking questions such as:

- What are your strongest departments?
- How many undergraduates do you admit each year?
- Which sports teams have the best reputations in their leagues?

Those who ask for facts may think this demonstrates serious interest in the school, but there are two good reasons to avoid it:

1. It's redundant: The facts are usually spelled out in the school's literature, which the interviewer has read and will expect you to have read as well. If your questions reveal a lack of basic knowledge, that works against you.
2. It's boring: Your interviewer has many other students to interview as well. If everyone asks factual questions, the interviewer has to recite the same answers hundreds of times in a season. It gets tiring, and the last thing you want is a bored interviewer.

My school paper won awards, and I can tell you why. I know because I was there. I worked on the paper every day that summer. I held staff meetings even during vacations and on weekends. I came in early, and I stayed late, and I edited every word to make sure we had a top quality newspaper.

When I read his draft, I told him, "You haven't said anything about leadership."

"What do you mean?" he asked. "I was in charge of the paper that summer, and I made sure everything got done right."

"That shows that you worked long and hard," I said. "Hard work is admirable. But it's not leadership because there's no one in your story but you. It sounds like you were a one-man band. Is that true?"

A yearbook editor, Paula, also worked hard, but in her story she reflected on why her team was successful. She was very critical when she started as editor, because she thought that quick, clear judgments would get people to take her seriously. But over time she changed her approach. "I tried to get kids working constructively for each other rather than competing against each other, and discovered that encouragement and confidence in others beats being judgmental, every time."

However much you may feel you accomplished in high school, it's worth remembering that you will never be in high school again. Colleges know that, and they hope to see what you'll bring with you besides memories: the way you think (intellectual orientation—are you open to ideas different from your own?), the ways you work with others, your ambitions. Your past accomplishments as a leader are less significant for the future than the approach you take to leadership itself.

Dangerous Topics in Leadership Essays

Here are ways I'd encourage you *not* to try to demonstrate your potential as a leader in your essays.

1. **Lists of achievements.** Admissions committees have your application handy, so they already know your grades and any honors or leadership positions you may have won. Listing these in an essay takes up space and risks giving the impression that you have an immature understanding of leadership. Although it can be useful to go into detail about one or two leadership experiences, listing your leadership positions like pieces of evidence is not helpful.

2. **Expressions of pleasure or gratitude that you were chosen as a leader.** Just about everyone who is given a leadership role or title feels good about it. Again and again, I see students write

STEPS TO SUCCESS

Leadership means asserting yourself to help others have more success. There are chances to contribute in class, in the dorms and in extracurriculars, whether you are outgoing or shy. Find the kinds of leadership that suit you—and let the colleges know how you can contribute.

about how they "were filled with happiness to be selected" or "deeply honored to be chosen by the team/the group/the toad-lovers' club." There is nothing wrong with such feelings, but they show your essay readers very little they wouldn't have guessed. Save these descriptions for your acceptance speeches, and leave room in your college essays to go deeper.

3. **The drama of your wilderness leadership course.** If you go on one, it may seem like your experience would make a good essay topic. Won't your readers share in your excitement? The answer is, probably not. For one thing, these courses are so common now that most admissions people have read dozens of essays about them. And for another, because these courses are actually vacations you pay to go on, you are not actually left to starve in the wilderness or fight off marauding bears. So although it felt dramatic at the time, your readers already know how the story ends: You make it out alive, you get home safely, and then you apply to college. If you do write about a leadership training course, be sure to keep your focus on what you were discovering about leadership, and not the apparent drama of whether the castaways would survive.

CHAPTER FIVE

FATAL MISTAKE #5

You Seem Like a Threat

Beware this error if . . .

—*You have a competitive streak; you like to be the best*
—*You're known for your sharp tongue*
—*When you see trouble, you don't get involved*

Imagine this: You are asked to pick one of two strangers from the grade below you to spend the night at your house. The kid you pick will eat dinner with your family, use all your things, share your bathroom, and sleep right down the hall. In the morning you'll go to class together. One of these kids is talented and smart and seems responsible. The other one is talented and smart but seems like a selfish, impulsive third-grader. Which one do you choose?

Okay, maybe you invite the brat, because it's just one night and he could be good for a laugh, driving your family crazy. But now imagine he isn't just staying for one night. He's staying for four years. And he's bringing a few hundred—or a few thousand—of his friends. For the rest of his life, he'll display a bumper sticker with your family name on it. Oh, and one other thing: Making this choice is your new job, and your family will kick you out if the kids you pick trash your house.

Now, which one do you choose?

Welcome to the perspective of an admissions person. Their job is not just to consider what each candidate can contribute to the community, it's also to prevent what we might call "antileadership": acts that hurt the community, that spoil classmates' experiences and hurt their chances for success. Preventing antileadership is at least as important as finding leaders. Consider again that imaginary choice I gave you between two kids to invite to your house. If you thought that one was a real threat to your family or your home, wouldn't you pick the other kid right then and there, no matter who seemed smarter or more talented?

Colleges are always on the lookout for threats to their community, and the admissions committee is their first line of defense. So while you're readying your applications and wondering how your scores and activities compare to someone else's, admissions committees are trying to figure out if you might do harm.

MAYBE YOU DON'T FEEL LIKE A THREAT

So what, really? You don't think of yourself as a threat, do you? I'll bet it's hard for you to imagine that you could scare an admissions person. So let me tell you what I've observed:

1. You don't have to be an actual threat for this mistake to do you in. It's bad enough if colleges worry that you *might* do harm. They would rather be safe than sorry, and as I showed in Chapter One, they only have a brief chance to get to know you. Sometimes they reject students who only give the appearance of being a possible threat.

2. Most applicants who set off warning lights in the minds of admissions officers never know they tripped an alarm. It's not as if they walk in swinging nunchakus like a ninja assassin, ex-

pecting fear in their interviewer's eyes. Even after receiving rejection letters, students perceived as threats often don't know what they did wrong.

So how do you keep from setting off their alarms, when colleges may get alarmed for no discernible reason, and you probably won't know it if they do? You need to understand what they look for when they're picking the "kid" who will live at their "house."

WHAT ARE THEY SO AFRAID OF? AGGRESSION

First I'll give you an extreme example of an applicant who set off alarms, because his story makes the issue of harm to the community very clear. Once you have seen more blatant examples, I'll show you how to recognize subtler examples of the same threats.

Here is part of an essay by a student who imagined he was showing the college valuable qualities of competition and loyalty. He felt confident enough to send the essay in without letting anyone see it. His mother showed me the essay after he was rejected for early decision at his first-choice school.

> I have a learning disability, and that may sound like a disadvantage, but I make it work for me. When it makes me angry and frustrated, I get rid of my anger toward my teachers by pounding the ball past my opponents on the tennis court. As a player on the school tennis team, that anger is really my secret weapon.
>
> Once, I played in a match where my opponent was the heavy favorite. He had been arrogant to me in the past, and before this match he was arrogant to me again. Early on, he came to the net, and I hit the ball right between his eyes. It was at close range, but I thought he would probably duck.

After he was hit, he didn't seem to be hurt badly. I apologized, but secretly I enjoyed hitting him. And that sudden rush energized me to play my best and pull an upset. To be honest, he was probably a little woozy from the blow, and that probably didn't help his game. Still, for the team's sake, I had to go for the kill.

The author of this essay was proud of what he'd written. Even after his rejection, he told me, "I don't see what their problem is. I showed character, just like you said—honesty, toughness, competitiveness, and team spirit. Isn't that what they want?"

He was half right. Colleges want students who will be strong and assertive in the pursuit of doing their best. They want the spirited and the ambitious. But among the ambitious, they want those who strive to excel in ways that don't do harm. This student had been honest about his emotional impulses, and those impulses were very human. His fatal mistake wasn't in having violent impulses. His mistake was in failing to recognize that his impulses could harm others, and that admissions people wouldn't be sure he had the maturity to control those impulses. As I said, this is an extreme example, but it shows one of an admissions person's worst nightmares: an applicant who would do harm to get ahead.

Here is a less violent, though no less serious, example of the same kind of threat. Marni was a top student in her class and one of the stars of the debating club. She always had a strong counterargument and a sharp retort, and she was one of the reasons the club had done well in competitions. Her style was aggressive, and she was known for ridiculing those who debated against her. Her combination of skill and insults was often an effective debate technique at the high school level. Her aggressive style appeared nowhere on her record, but one of her teachers—in fact, a teacher who'd given her an A—mentioned in her recommendation letter that Marni carried her aggressive debating style into the classroom. The result was rejection in eight out of eight applications.

Why? Although the admissions people may have admired her debating successes, their responsibility was to keep out a potential cutthroat who would intimidate other students and shut down discussions. Open discussion makes a liberal arts education possible, and a person who seems to threaten it simply doesn't fit. As one commenter observed, "That just isn't the sort of person we want to see every day."

Marni would have been more attractive to colleges if she had found ways to express her natural competitiveness that were less demeaning and destructive toward others. It's fine to want to win, but never at the expense of the dignity of an opponent. Why are football players resented by their opponents when they perform victory dances in the end zone? Because players on the other team feel put down. Marni went a step further: She was mean. Colleges want competitive people, but not aggressive ones, who need to lower someone else to win.

If you're still with me, let's look at a subtler version. One applicant who was chosen to write the senior-class skit included an impression of a teacher who stuttered. The skit was funny in the style of a mean-spirited television comedy, and the teacher, who was in the audience, got upset and had to leave the building. When confronted later by the guidance counselor, the student refused to apologize, saying that the skit was funny and he expected an adult to be confident enough to be able to take some kidding. But to admissions people hearing about the incident, it sounded like a dangerous lack of judgment, and lack of empathy. Humor that wounds a person, particularly in one's own community, is a form of aggression.

WHAT DOES THIS
HAVE TO DO WITH YOU?

Maybe you read this and you think, "I don't bean my fellow students with tennis balls or humiliate teachers with withering insults.

What does this have to do with me?" The answer is that the colleges are so concerned about aggression that they are wary of it in even very small amounts. And because they have only a short time to get to know each applicant, sometimes a seemingly innocent remark or a nervous impulse can be enough to raise the alarm. In other words, you don't have to be an aggressive person to raise concerns. After all, applying to schools in itself is enough to make anyone feel tense, irritable, and even kind of hostile sometimes. Interviews can bring out some nervousness, and even punchiness, in everybody. So be aware that you may feel provoked at times. Just as people going through airport security may feel tempted to joke about bombs, students who feel scrutinized and tested by a college may have the impulse to make hostile or defensive jokes that can set off warning lights in an admissions person's mind. I can think of two students who became angry in college interviews and lost out as a result. One was a Southerner who felt insulted by a query about Southern racism and the other was a football player who was asked why he thought football should be allotted so much importance in an academic community.

The Southerner took offense, which might have been warranted, but his response was over the top. Afterward, he told me, "I almost went over the table to get the guy." So at least we know he showed open hostility. The football player, who was a straight-A student who eventually became a Rhodes scholar, just froze. He fumbled around with some references to school spirit and revenue for the athletic department. Both went on the defensive, when the best approach would have been to ask the interviewer what his views were and then diplomatically and objectively disagree. You can always disagree if you first acknowledge that the other person has some good points, but then with a very pleasant, even amused expression, you give your own point of view. All these interviewers were looking for was poise and objectivity. You can't lose your cool or completely retreat. Always show respect for the other person's point of view and then, calmly and pleasantly, give your own.

DANGER SIGN: *You want to be "the best"*

How does it sound to an admissions committee when you say you want to be the best at what you do, the top of the class, number one?

Different from what you might expect. It's unlikely to inspire their admiration. From their point of view, the school has many talented, hardworking students—many more than in your high school—and so your odds of being the best are actually tiny. What will you do, they worry, when you realize you probably can't top everyone at everything? Will you have the maturity to accept being one of many talented students? Or will you become a threat to your fellow students by cheating, damaging their work, or taking out your competitive feelings by means of aggression or harm to yourself?

NEVER ELEVATE YOURSELF
BY PUTTING OTHERS DOWN

Let's consider some subtler forms of aggression, starting with this excerpt from an essay: "I have a job in a pharmacy all day, every Saturday and Sunday, while my friends are out riding around town in their sports cars, hitting the beach and smoking pot. My parents aren't bad off, but I feel a responsibility to earn my own money." What's the big deal? After all, isn't this student showing a strong sense of personal responsibility? Yes, but he's doing it by insulting the character and good citizenship of his peers, calling them spoiled lawbreakers.

You might respond, "Come on, that's stretching it." But in fact, admissions people with whom I discussed this student told me they saw this as a clear case. The feedback I heard was: This is a problem. He's making accusations against his fellow competitors, and they have no chance to defend themselves. He's trying to build himself up by tearing them down. In effect, he's tripping the other runners in his race. One reaction was: "Don't leave your lab reports unattended while this kid is around."

Now, could the essay readers know for sure that this kid was a bully and a thief? No, they couldn't. Maybe he was neither. Maybe the writer had good reason to resent his classmates on the beach. But he expressed himself in his essay the way the killer tennis player played tennis, willing to hit his fellow students when they were undefended. This made him *seem* like a bully, and it left him open to a negative reading from the admissions committee.

A TEST OF YOUR MATURITY AND LOYALTY: HOW DO YOU RESPOND TO IMMATURITY AROUND YOU?

Colleges are not only on the lookout for harm you might possibly do, but for your response when others do harm. Once, I worked at a school where a student drug dealer was arrested. As he was escorted off campus by school administrators and the police, a crowd of students followed, tearfully offering sad good-byes to the student under

---

STEPS TO SUCCESS: *Criticism*

When you criticize someone in an essay or an interview, strive for a tone of respect toward the person with whom you find fault. There is a world of difference between "I'd like to be part of a student body that really challenges me" and "At my school the kids are dumb as turtles." Similarly, your first thought might be "My headmaster is a total control freak," but you'll seem less aggressive if you say something like "I'm looking forward to the independence of college life." By expressing criticism without going on the attack, you show respect for another's dignity. To colleges, this is a hugely important personal quality.

INTERVIEW FIRST AID: *Threatening remarks*

What if you feel like you can't avoid saying something really harsh in an essay or interview?

Show that you can distinguish between feelings and actions. Everyone has a dark side, but you can help colleges recognize that there is more than one side to you. You can say, "I feel this way sometimes, but intellectually I can see that I like my other side far better." Then show that you recognize the different sides of yourself and make the most mature and sensitive response possible. In an interview, Matt said, "I know I just said my principal was a total jerk, but I was not being very fair, because the principal has his strong points. I'm just angry at him right now. He's really a good principal, I just think he's closed-minded on an issue that mattered to me. He fired a teacher who maybe expressed his political views a little too strongly, but he was a great history teacher who taught me a lot about writing. Nevertheless, I guess I can now see something of the principal's side. He has his strong points." You can usually bounce back from an aggressive remark by offering a more balanced point of view.

---

arrest. One student in the crowd, Sandra, was so moved by the experience that she wrote an essay about it:

> I don't understand why. This boy was our classmate and friend. Why does the school have to report drug users to the police? Aren't we a family? Shouldn't we enforce school rules ourselves? Besides, shouldn't academic institutions stand up to the law when it encroaches on a school's privacy?

Normally, admissions committees value students who explore the philosophical questions suggested by their own lives, and appreciate an applicant who craves justice and truth. Nevertheless, this essay set off alarms. Friend or no, a drug dealer is an illegal and dangerous presence at a high school, and the school has a responsibility to uphold the law, protect its students, and preserve its good name. When Sandra suggested that school administrators should "stand up to the law" to protect the kid who dealt drugs, she was only thinking about what this person meant to her and her circle of friends. She was not thinking about what was good for the school community. An admissions person could only wonder: What other rules would she think didn't apply to her friends? What other dangers to the community would she tolerate?

Every school hopes that its students will stand up for the law and the good of the school. Even if you go to a high school where students fear social isolation or worse if they speak out, there is often a system of intermediaries such as peer counselors or a school psychologist you can speak to safely.

I do not mean to suggest, by the way, that there isn't room for different opinions about drugs and their legality. This experience might have been a good place to start for an essay on that topic. However, if Sandra wanted to write an essay about how this experience made her think about how a school is like a family, or whether current drug laws were correct, then I'd have suggested that she say clearly that the experience raised a more philosophical question, and also say just as clearly that she didn't think the solution was to break the law. In this way she could have shown balance—that she was an independent thinker—without scaring off colleges concerned about her tolerance for rule-breaking and student crime.

PROTECTING THE COMMUNITY IN ESSAYS AND INTERVIEWS

Colleges often ask direct questions to learn how applicants might treat their communities. Many applications include essay questions about cheating or about the school honor code, if there is one. In response, many students make statements that may be well-intentioned but wind up sounding obvious, egotistical, and morally childish. Anyone can write the words "I believe in your honor code" or "I don't cheat on tests." Intensifying these statements is no help. ("I respect your honor code and I believe in it and I'll always follow it, cross my heart. . . .") So what can you do if these statements are true, but you want to be convincing?

This is one of those cases where a good offense is the best defense. If you have already acted to prevent Fatal Mistakes #1, #2, and #3, then the schools already see you as a lover of learning who is ready and eager to contribute to the community. Generosity, maturity, and intellectual enthusiasm are the natural antidotes to aggression and cheating. Your high school record and teacher recommendation letters will speak for themselves to display your unselfish acts and intellectual passion.

Therefore if the subject of loyalty to your school and honor codes comes up in an interview or in an essay question, show that you can go beyond promising to follow the rules. Show that you understand the *reasons* behind the rules against cheating and aggression, and the harm that a student can do to the community if he or she makes destructive choices.

WHOM DOES CHEATING HARM?

I remember one student, Alix, who wrote the following: "I can't wait to be in a place where there is no cheating, so that I won't be taken advantage of by students who know less than myself." In this statement, Alix sounds as if she thinks the main problem with cheating is what she herself loses. When another student cheats off of her test, it changes her place on the grading curve. She's not wrong, but she seems to suggest that cheating is not a moral issue, only a practical one. In a similar vein, another student wrote, "I would never cheat, because that would be cheating myself." He was not wrong either. Cheating does hurt him personally. It hurts his own integrity and sense of his own goodness. But the colleges want to know if students' concern about cheating extends beyond their own self-interest, to take in the harm it does to others. Again, they want to know: Are students only out for themselves, or are they also looking out for their school community?

For this reason, schools tend not to be impressed by angry essays about other students who cheat. They see cheating as another situation that cries out for strong leadership and social responsibility. "Why couldn't this student take more of a leadership role?" they are likely to ask. "Why couldn't he become a peer counselor or, if that role doesn't exist in his community, work with the school counseling support system to attack the issue? Why didn't he fight for the integrity of his school?" In stories of cheating observed, colleges keep their eye on the observer. Faced with a moral choice, did the student stand up and confront the cheating, or did he let it go? As one of Alix's admission readers responded, "She wants us to protect her against dishonesty? Where is her courage?" To the colleges, if you witness cheating, the responsibility is on you to show your character in your response.

HARM TO ONE IS HARM TO ALL

Colleges are on the lookout for harm that is intentional, like using ridicule to win debates, and also harm that's unintentional, like failing to think about how a drug dealer might endanger a school. They are even concerned about students who seem solitary and isolated. Why? The concern here is emotional vulnerability. Every college has serious concerns about drug and alcohol abuse. Every school must face the possibility of a certain percentage of students who give up on themselves. When a student goes down a self-destructive path, it's hard not only on the student who's suffering, but his roommates, his dorm-mates and his friends, and the faculty who know him. In the more serious cases, the entire school may feel the blow.

It is difficult to predict which students might conceivably have problems with drugs or alcohol, or who might try to do themselves harm, but active, sociable kids are thought to be at lower risk. Participation in the arts, sports, organized religion, or social causes are all thought to correlate with greater happiness and emotional stability. For these reasons, college interviewers tend to ask some seemingly bland questions:

"Would you describe yourself as an active person?"

"What are your friends like?"

"What do you like to do with your free time?"

For some students, it can be tempting to answer these seemingly dull questions in a casual way. In response to the questions about what they do with free time, I've known students to give answers like:

"Sometimes."

"They're cool; they like to be together."

"Nothing much. Hang out."

Such answers may mean nothing more than that the student hasn't really stopped to think about what fills his or her free time, and yet the lack of any reliable enjoyable activities may sound to the schools like trouble. So whatever you like to do, you should be ready to talk about what you do in your free time, no matter what your activities are. You may love camping, skateboarding, reading for pleasure, bungee jumping, gardening, yodeling, golfing, or rodeo competitions. What colleges want to know is that leisure time is not just used for solitary vegetating. Of course, we all have times when we just want to collapse on the couch—and at the end of a college interview, that may be primarily what's on your mind. Make sure, therefore, you're prepared to give the schools a sense of your activities or activeness, to reassure them. "Well-rounded" is irrelevant to them. You could be a figure skater working at it ten hours a day, just as long as you are not inactive. Colleges don't even like the concept of well-rounded. Contrary to what many people think, it is a good term to avoid. It suggests you are a dabbler and not exceptional at nor deeply interested in anything.

For the same reason, American colleges (more than any other nation's) care greatly about whether you will be happy. They often ask,

STEPS TO SUCCESS

R eassure schools that you're not a threat.

How?

- • Avoid showing them evidence of your outright aggression, whether physical or verbal.
- • Avoid harsh humor and raising yourself up by putting others down.
- • Show your understanding of the ways that schools depend on their students' loyalty and commitment.
- • Emphasize your ability to connect with others.

"Where do you think you'll find your niche at our school?" They ask not just because they're nice people like your great-aunt Mildred and great-uncle Bert, who hope you'll have a nice visit. They ask because they know that you will have to find that niche yourself, that place where you seem to fit in and thrive.

Is this the leadership issue again? No. This time, their focus isn't on what you can do to help others succeed. This time, they want to know what you can do to help yourself succeed and enjoy your college experience. They want to make sure that you will feel fulfilled in their community, which increases the odds that you will be a contributor, and not a threat.

CHAPTER SIX

FATAL MISTAKE #6

Social Insensitivity

Beware of this error if . . .

> —*You don't see what a social conscience has to do with getting into college*

In an interview, one of my counselees was asked what he cared about most, socially. "Socially?" he said. "I like to party. Hang out with my friends, relax. You know. If the weather's good, we go down to the lake. . . ."

Maybe it was the generation gap between him and his interviewer that made the word *social* confusing, but he didn't realize that this wasn't a question about his social life. It was a question about his social conscience—his level of caring about other people. It's a common interview question, but my counselee, like a surprising number of applicants, didn't understand it right away. Once he did, he was under pressure to show that his world extended farther than the next party.

Why should a social conscience matter to an admissions committee? After all, they're taking applications for a school, not a charity. The answer goes back, partly, to Chapter Five: If you demonstrate a social conscience, that suggests you will not be a threat to your fellow students or to your school. It makes you seem like a safer member of the community. However, there is another reason. When you try out for a sports team, the coach wants to know what you're capable of: How fast can you run? How high can you jump? In the same way, colleges want to know about your mental capacities, and one of these is moral imagination. We all know, pretty well, how to look out for ourselves, our friends, and our families. Many of us have developed our imaginations enough to see, at least sometimes, through the eyes of the people we are close to. It takes more, though, to imagine what someone else's experience is like when that person is *unlike* you. Are you able to empathize with someone else's anguish? Can you think about what's just and fair for people you don't know personally?

Let's take an example. Suppose for a moment that you are one of America's top teen sumo wrestlers. You weigh six hundred pounds, you receive adoring fan mail from sumo fans in Japan and around the world, and you have high hopes of receiving a wrestling scholarship for college. You also find it difficult to go to the mall and eat at the food court, because the seats are too small. Mall designers and restaurant owners have failed to provide for the needs of the sumo wrestling population. One day, in fact, as you walk through the mall, you see another amateur American sumo wrestler trying to have a slice of pizza while sitting on a narrow stool. As you watch, the stool collapses, and your fellow wrestler is embarrassed and mildly bruised. You are so upset by seeing a fellow sumo suffering that you decide to write your personal statement for college about the experience, and how you came to recognize the deep unfairness of food-court seating design.

Is this a good example of moral imagination?

No. Not only is it a goofy example, it does not demonstrate any moral imagination. For you, a sumo wrestler, understanding how another sumo wrestler feels in a situation that you yourself have experienced and know well is hardly thinking beyond yourself at all. You two wrestlers are as alike, at least physically, as any two people could be. On the other hand, if you wrote about a jockey who was too short to climb up onto the stools at the mall's Chinese restaurant, then at least you would show, as someone larger than average, that you could *imagine the experience* of being someone smaller than average. That is how you show social sensitivity: Through your imagination, you walk in the shoes of someone unlike yourself.

WHO NEEDS MORAL IMAGINATION?

But wait, you may be thinking. Moral imagination may be nice, even admirable, but as a practical collegiate skill, is it really a top priority? It might matter for humanities majors and those with people-oriented career goals: nurses, social workers, psychologists, novelists, teachers, and so forth. But these capacities aren't essential for the rest of us, are they?

In fact, from the point of view of the colleges, they are essential across the professions: for lawyers and those in law enforcement who deal every day in right and wrong; for doctors and other scientists who must imagine the experience of their patients and subjects; for engineers who have to care about the long-term durability of the structures they design; and for people in business, who affect the financial security of others. In the past few years, the business world, for instance, has been shaken by one major scandal after another—from Enron to Tyco, and the list goes on. Respect for businesspeople has tanked. Business schools are asking the colleges, what kind of young people are you sending us? Do they have the moral imagination to think about what's right and wrong in business?

For these reasons, admissions committees look for signs of a flourishing moral imagination. Any aspect of your application is fair game for scrutiny. We had one applicant who wrote an essay about the Lewis and Clark expedition, which he considered an inspiring story of exploration and courage. That was fine, of course, and it was impressive that he had read accounts of the expedition written back then, and not just histories from the present day. But in describing the expedition across our young country, he got into trouble. The group of explorers was made up of predominantly white men and white and Native American women, but it also included one African-American male slave. Now, at that time, a black slave did not enjoy the legal status of a "man," and when writers of the time counted up the "men" on the expedition, they left this man out. When my student described the number of male explorers, he did not count the slave among the males in the group either. He wrote about twelve men instead of thirteen, following right along with the dehumanizing ethos of that distant era.

What was the result? This boy appeared naïve at best. "Wow, this kid is out of touch with millions of people in his own country" was one reader's response. Another followed with more sympathy: "I'm sure it was an honest mistake, but those are the kinds of mistakes that hurt people."

WHAT IF SOCIAL SENSITIVITY ISN'T YOUR THING?

Some students I've worked with get uncomfortable about this issue. Moral imagination, they feel, isn't their thing. "You say it's like being able to jump high or run fast," one student told me, "but I'm not going out for sports either. Is this sensitivity thing really so important to my application?"

That question made me remember my days as a high school's college counselor. There was one excellent women's college we often recommended, but our young women would not apply there. They came back from their visits saying, "Everyone at that school is a lesbian!" Eventually I visited the school. It was true, there was a visible presence of women who seemed to be dating other women, but statistically, at that time, only seven percent of the student body identified themselves as lesbian. Our kids had obviously exaggerated their findings. So I spoke to the director of admissions and told her that some students at my school were afraid they wouldn't be comfortable at her college. She said, "All it takes for a heterosexual to be happy here is tolerance."

Tolerance is one of the foundations of American college life. Schools don't just value tolerance because they think it's morally admirable. Most colleges rely on tolerance in order to function day to day. That's because a college campus is a very unusual mix of two different kinds of communities. Like a city, it brings together people from many different places, with many different lives. But like a small town, it expects those people to work together, social-ize together, as they bump up against one another every day. Liberal arts colleges can't survive without a tolerant student body, and so they screen for social sensitivity. If students can imagine and re-spect the experience of those unlike themselves, then the student body, however varied and challenging, will likely find a way to get along.

WHAT IF YOU HAVE
STRONG OPINIONS?

As I've said, my emphasis on social sensitivity makes some appli-cants nervous. "I have strong opinions," one of our counselees told me. "I call 'em like I see 'em. That's how I was brought up. Does that make me socially insensitive?"

He wasn't kidding about his strong opinions. For his personal statement, he wrote a scathing and one-sided essay against affirma-tive action. He called it "unequivocal racism in reverse." Now, he was an exceptional student, and a track star recruited by an Ivy League school. Even so, if this essay seemed to be all the moral imagination he could muster, I was afraid he could expect summary rejection. I told him I had some concerns about the essay. He shot back, "Yeah? Well, I have some concerns about prejudice against kids from affluent white families."

It didn't seem like we would get anywhere by arguing, so I told him a story. Once when I was working in my office in Boston, a young African-American high school senior walked in off the street. This young woman told me that she had never seen a book in her home. There was no adult around to encourage her to study until late at night. At her school, the teachers' first priority was their own physical safety—violent threats against teachers were common. However, despite her antiacademic surroundings, this young woman had a solid, if not extraordinary, academic record. And it was easy to imagine she would be capable of much more under better circumstances. For that reason, in fact, I took her on as a client for free.

When my counselee heard this story, he began for the first time to look at the other side of the affirmative action argument, imagining the life experiences (far from his own) and social problems that had inspired the creation of affirmative action as a solution. He didn't change his mind, but that hadn't been my goal. I knew he might still disagree with its philosophy or the way the policy was put into action, but at least he could begin now to imagine the perspective of the people who held a view different from his own. And when he revised his essay, the admissions committee could see in it a potential for flexible thinking and compassion.

HOW TO DEVELOP
YOUR MORAL IMAGINATION

Of all the character qualities I talk about, I've noticed that social sensitivity is the most likely to make people nervous. Students I speak with may feel unfairly tested or criticized when I ask them about it. "What are you saying?" a few want to know. "Are the schools going to think I'm a bad person?"

It's certainly true that for some people, social sensitivity seems to come naturally, while for others, it takes commitment and time to develop. But this is true for every character quality, and indeed almost every human capacity or skill. Some runners have great form the first time they try to run a long distance; others need to be coached. Some kids seem to teach themselves to read with little or no instruction from adults; others need several years of school or tutoring. But almost everyone can learn to complete a 5K race or read a book (or listen to one on tape). In the same way, a social conscience (like all character qualities) is something virtually everyone can develop.

Again, social sensitivity doesn't mean just being polite or respectful toward people unlike yourself. It means that you have developed your ability to think beyond yourself and the people closest to you, to begin to see from other people's perspectives. If you feel unprepared to talk about social issues, I'll lead you through a progression of self-study questions to help you tap into your moral imagination.

Try asking yourself these questions, jotting down whatever comes to mind and then returning to them later and adding to your notes. The point here is not to write an essay or even find an essay topic (though you might wind up with ideas), it's just to "exercise" your moral imagination and get you more comfortable with these sorts of questions.

Whom would you define as "your group" or "your circle"?

Do your friends ever talk about people outside that circle?

Do you ever read or see movies about people outside that circle?

What are some surprising differences or similarities you've noticed about the lives of people who seemed unlike you?

Can you think of a time when you found a common bond with someone who seemed, on the surface, utterly different?

Can you think of a time when you felt deeply about people you had no personal connection to at all?

If you allow yourself time to work through this progression of questions, you may find that your perspective begins to shift. I saw this happen with a young woman who spent her junior year abroad and then came home to write an essay about her adventures in learning the native language. After four months living and studying in Spain, she wrote, she reached the point where she could finally understand the day-to-day chat of her hosts. For her application essay, she wrote a colorful description of how she bonded with her dynamic, loving family in a foreign tongue. However, in her first draft of this essay, she only gave the reader a clever story about sumptuous meals, jolly singing festivals, and occasionally awkward misunderstandings. The essay was charmingly written, but it shared nothing of her response to encountering these people who were unlike herself. In writing her essay, she'd assumed that just being able to say she'd lived in a foreign country would seem "socially sensitive" and impress her readers. She was half right; her interaction with her adopted family and their friends spoke volumes about her social ability. But it revealed nothing about how her travels sparked her own thinking.

What difference did it make, I asked her, to have these conversations that she'd worked so hard to have? Was she surprised at what they talked about or how it mattered to her? Was she changed at all by the culture of such a different place?

In her next draft, she wrote:

> In my adopted home, we continuously debated the pros and cons of capitalism and socialism. Although we sometimes intensely disagreed, the talk stayed friendly because we all liked each other from the time before I could speak well enough to talk politics. We all wanted to get along, and I was amazed how much less rigid in our positions we all became because of our friendship. It made me think of how important it is to have personal encounters with the people I disagree with, or with whom I would seem to have so little in common.

With this conclusion, she showed not only that she could learn to communicate in a foreign language, but that she had the social sensitivity to flourish in that situation and to grow personally.

SHOWING EMPATHY
IN YOUR APPLICATION

Course grades and test scores don't tend to reveal moral imagination. The one area that might is the list of your extracurricular activities. When I meet with parents, they often ask me about how to expand their children's experience in social service, believing that colleges want to see some tangible evidence of social conscience. Sometimes, those with the means ask me if they should send their applicants to one- or two-week social service programs in developing countries. But while some parents focus on signing their kids up for short-term social programs, colleges look more at a young person's social spirit. They are looking for "heart," and they find it when they see a pattern of involvement, not just an isolated effort or two. They are looking for depth and length of commitment that suggest that the student doesn't just want to feel good about him- or herself, but has a real passion for understanding and being of service to others. In this sense, admissions committees are looking to see whether social service is a "hot area" for you, a moral passion comparable to the intellectual passions described earlier.

For example, everyone knew Randi in her boarding school community. She was everywhere, it seemed, holding out a carton to raise money for Oxfam's efforts to end world hunger. During school vacations, moreover, she worked for other organizations with the same goal. She even convinced her school debate team, of which she was a member, to make world hunger the basis for the topics when her school hosted an intramural debate competition. Because of her extraordinary commitment to this goal and in spite of modest SAT scores, her first-choice college wanted her. It was her level of passion and degree of personal sacrifice that so impressed them.

REVISING THE RULE

~~To show your social sensitivity, list your social service activities and the foreign places you have visited.~~
To show your social sensitivity, demonstrate your ongoing commitment to learning about and responding to the experiences of people unlike yourself.

So should you participate in programs for the disadvantaged in faraway places? These are noble activities, and if your family can afford them, I say, "Terrific." On the other hand, since they are not a financial option for most families, they will cause participants to stand out not as socially committed but as privileged. Benevolent projects such as midnight food runs to needy areas close to home are just as valuable, and I encourage them, too, if they seem worthwhile and are something you believe in. But from the point of view of college applications, understand that a short-lived commitment to helping others will seem just like it sounds: a short-lived commitment. To make a difference in your application profile, you need to show a deep commitment to a cause that consumes a substantial amount of time.

However, a short experience can matter to a college if it has an ongoing effect on your thinking, which you can demonstrate in an interview or an essay.

Showing Empathy in the Interview

A high school ice hockey star was asked the following question: "How do you justify spending so much of your time on this . . . game?"

"I don't think of hockey as something I need to justify. It's my sport," he said.

"Come on," said the interviewer. "It's an animal sport. It's like cockfighting, or bearbaiting. Pure animal aggression out there on display, and for what? What good does it do, really? You seem like a pretty smart kid. How do you justify using your time like that?"

The applicant got angry. In the end, he raised his voice at the interviewer and left before his time was up. The interview had not gone well.

Afterward, the hockey player called me, upset. I sympathized. The questions had been provocative and they'd hurt his feelings.

"Why would he go after me like that?" the young athlete asked. "Doesn't he know that his alums want a winning team?"

I told him I did think that this interviewer knew that hockey was important to his school. But I also suggested that rather than being a simple personal attack, this line of questioning might have been a test to find out how he would respond to someone who didn't share his affinity for competitive sports or see the world in general as he did, from an athlete's perspective. In other words, he'd given this student a chance to show his social sensitivity—a chance the student had blown.

What else could he have done? My best advice is: Try to enjoy your interviewer. If she seems weird, try to enjoy her weirdness as a short vacation from the usual. If he is aggressive, try to admire his guts at least a little. You don't have to agree with your interviewer's perspective, but at the very least, you can laugh. You can say, "I never looked at it that way!"

It's worth mentioning that provocative questions don't always come from the interviewer's side. Insensitive student questions can also produce tension and even anger in an interview. One privileged counselee of ours was interviewing at her safety school when she discovered to her surprise that the interviewer, who had grown up as an inner-city, disadvantaged minority, did not share her interest in polo. He knew nothing about the sport, nor had he skied in the winter or enjoyed scuba diving in the Caribbean. The only traveling abroad he had ever done was paid for by the college. He remembered missing one question on the SAT test because he did not know what a tablecloth was. On the other hand, the college was well known for its riding program, so our candidate asked:

"Why don't you offer polo here?"

"How do you imagine we have the financial resources to offer such an expensive sport for the very few privileged kids who would participate?" was the response.

"You have horses, don't you?" she answered.

We had to find her another safety.

POLITICAL QUESTIONS

Another favorite interview question is "What social issues, either domestic or international, concern you the most?" Here, the admissions person is assuming that if your moral imagination is awake, you will naturally begin to notice events in the news that concern and engage you. In my experience, this is true, but not everyone follows the news regularly enough, or talks enough about current events, to answer such a question off the cuff. If you can't name two or three issues right now, or if you don't feel you could explain why such issues concern you, I suggest you begin to read one of the following publications once a week, looking for the stories that interest you and get you thinking about the experience of people both like and unlike yourself:

The Sunday **New York Times** *"Week in Review" section*

The Wall Street Journal

The Economist

Newsweek *or* **Time**

I recommend reading rather than watching television because written news sources have more time to explain the background of an issue, and to go into personal stories that make the issues understandable and compelling. Also, it's easier to save and review articles than news programs. And, of course, to a college interviewer, it's better to refer to what you've read rather than what you've seen on television.

Showing Empathy in the Essay

Some schools test your social sensitivity directly, with an essay question such as "What has prepared you to live in the kind of socially diverse community you will find at our school?" But even if they don't ask about it directly, all liberal arts schools look for this crucial quality in your essays. Any time that you write about an encounter with someone unlike yourself, you are giving an example of your moral imagination—how fully, and with how much respect and genuine interest, you can imagine other people's experiences. While I would not advise worrying about this while writing your first draft, when you go back and revise, it's worth asking yourself where you have put your focus. Are you empathetic toward those both like and unlike you?

Let me give an example. As it happened, one year I knew two American teenagers who traveled to the same third-world country to work in the same hospital. They did not know each other, and they were not there at the same time, but each had the same experience of coming from a rich country and encountering a poor one where many basic supplies and comforts were not available. When they came home, both students worked hard to write clear, well-organized essays about their experiences. One student wrote, "When I saw the absence of medical specialists and scarce medical treatment among the poor, plus the shortage of food, all I could think about was how fortunate I was. I suddenly appreciated my wonderful parents who had given me everything." Her focus was completely on herself, as if this foreign country only existed as a way for her to think about herself. She seemed to have no compassion for these terribly disadvantaged people.

STEPS TO SUCCESS

Show colleges that you have the moral imagination that will help you deal sensitively with people unlike yourself, whether they are down the hall from you, teaching your classes, or the subject of your studies.

How?

- Even if you have strong opinions, show that you can acknowledge two sides of an issue.
- Go to interviews ready to talk about some larger issues that have captured your imagination—something bigger than your personal life and your hopes for college.

In contrast, the other wrote, "The suffering among these people shocked me. Poverty was no longer an abstract idea, but a brutal reality. People's lips were stained orange from a beetle nut drug to lessen their pain from hunger. Trained doctors and nurses were scarce. In the hospital where I worked there were shortages of medicines and bandages. I felt good about myself just being there, but now it weighs on me that people with the most, like me, have to be more generous to people everywhere. We are responsible."

Now, I know that if you spend weeks or months in a foreign country, you will think many different things at different times about the places you see and the people you meet. Perhaps both of these students were capable of thinking not just about how lucky they were to have well-off parents, but also about the needs of those who were not so fortunate. Still, if you were an admissions officer with these two essays in front of you, all else being equal, which student would you take?

CHAPTER SEVEN

FATAL MISTAKE #7

Dependency

Beware this error if . . .

—*You feel uncomfortable sometimes offering your own ideas*
—*You show total dependence on your parents for every decision*
—*You like to do whatever the cool kids do*

The application for Grace's first-choice college asked for an essay on the question "Why are you applying to our school?" Grace began this way: "My parents and my teachers all agree that your university is the best place for me." In fact, when Grace chatted with her friends about the coming school year, she would begin sentences as if she had already been admitted. "When I go to X College next year . . ." she often said, appearing, to her friends, more interested in pleasing her parents than finding a good fit for herself. In her essay, she went on to give her parents' reasons, and to say that she agreed. Elsewhere in her application, she praised her parents, thanking them for "always guiding me and driving me to succeed." When Grace's parents heard from a friend that Grace seemed to rely on them so completely, they were surprised and disappointed; they had not intentionally infantilized Grace, but by the time they realized how far it had gone, it was too late.

How did the admissions committee respond? Not well. Grace's emphasis on what others thought, especially her parents' plans for her, raised a serious concern. The admissions people began to worry that Grace was too dependent on her parents to handle the challenges of college life. In the end, despite her impressive GPA and academic achievements, her first-choice school rejected her application. Why wasn't the admissions committee happy that she was a respectful young person who knew how to take advice? Well, perhaps they were. But those character qualities, however valid, are not tops on their wish list for a student body. Her answers raised a deeper concern: that Grace was too dependent on others to thrive in the liberal arts environment, where emotional and intellectual *independence* are a must. If she depended on others to make her academic commitments and frame her ideas, or if she studied hard because her family required it, what would happen when she left home? Were those fine character qualities hers—or theirs? I know this must sound crazy to some applicants and their parents. How can it be, they ask me, that excellent colleges don't appreciate the importance of strong families in student success? Why would they not treasure a student who is not only high-achieving but also modest enough to express gratitude to the family that did so much to help him or her achieve?

For other applicants, the risks of dependency may seem so obvious that they can't ever imagine committing this fatal error. How hard could it really be to show colleges your independent side? And yet Grace was, to my mind, a strong thinker. She'd researched her options thoroughly, read the school literature, visited the campuses, and talked to people in her town who had attended the schools she admired. Her decision was a mix of respectful listening and strong independent thinking, yet this college didn't seem to see it that way.

Each of us is a mix of dependence and independence, never more so than when we are teenagers. But what you need to know is that, from the point of view of the colleges, what often distinguishes the best students is independence that is *already well-developed*.

ARE YOU READY FOR THE FREEDOM OF COLLEGE?

I don't need to tell you that compared to your high school years, college will probably mean a whole lot more freedom. Less supervision, less structure to your day, and more opportunity to decide almost everything for yourself. Most likely you'll be away from home, but even if you still come home in the evenings, your school days will be far freer than before. No one will check on your attendance. No one will tell you when it's time to work. You'll most likely have unrestricted access to a town or city in which you will be a representative of your school: Whatever you do there, good, bad, or indifferent, local people will think, "That's how a kid from the college acts."

Academically, you will also have greater freedom. More choice about what to study and more chances to decide for yourself what is important. You'll pick your own courses, paper topics, and in time, your own major. (Of course, your parents may be involved in these choices, but you will be the one who ultimately registers for your classes and fills out the declaration of your major.) If you're used to letting others tell you what classes to take or what conclusions to draw, colleges will worry about how you'll react to being on your own. They want to know: Have you developed the inner resources to make good use of so much emotional and intellectual choice?

Of course, colleges don't expect complete independence. They know that most college applicants are still minors living at home. But they also know all too well the risks of taking in students who have not developed their independent sides. The impressive student who is overly dependent on family direction may collapse when left on his or her own, sometimes leading to depression and worse. The risk is particularly high in more traditional families, where the parents are often deeply involved in motivating and directing their children. As Dr. Soo Kim Abboud and Jane Kim point out in their book *Top of the Class*, children raised in traditional Asian families have unusually high rates of academic success—but also relatively high rates of collapse under pressure. The same is likely true for all traditional families that put an emphasis on achievement.

Admissions people are wary of overly dependent students not just for the students' sake, but for the school's sake as well. As they try to assemble a class of students with the character qualities I've been discussing, they also know that dependent students may appear to have those ideal qualities until they get out on their own. Sometimes these qualities come to resemble the changing colors of a chameleon confronted by a new environment. Here are some of the chameleonlike character qualities that often shift or change when overly dependent applicants must live as independent young adults:

Preparedness: *A student who is scheduled and directed by a family member may appear to be a well-organized, well-prepared applicant who knows how to pace his or her studies in order to enjoy them and excel. But if this preparedness comes from dependence on someone else, it may disappear when that student has to fly solo, revealing an unprepared, disorganized, and struggling college student.*

Intellectual Passion: *Students who follow someone else's direction may appear passionate about their studies until they are given more choice. Then they sometimes find not only that they have been studying the wrong things, but that they don't themselves know what they love, or even how to be sure of what intellectual passion feels like. Such formerly directed students may become confused and directionless.*

Threat to the School: *Some students who have put on a fake best self to please their families later go on to tear that fake self down with destructive behavior. They are more prone to cheat, to abuse drugs or alcohol, and to take out their anger in the form of vandalism. For the schools, it can seem that Dr. Jekyll applied, but Mr. Hyde showed up.*

Because the colleges have seen overly dependent students reveal their true colors later on, they want to be sure they aren't "fooled" in the application process. Appearing overly dependent is a fatal mistake because it makes admissions people question and even disregard exactly those qualities in you they would normally value.

And as with all "fatal mistakes," appearance counts. With only a short chance to get to know each applicant, admissions committees have to use the information they have to draw the best conclusion they can. Sometimes this means they confuse appearance with reality. My counselee Grace was not, in my opinion, too dependent emotionally to make a wise choice about her first-choice college. But she looked that way when she applied for early admission, and then it was too late.

DANGER: THE BALANCE TIPS TOWARD TOO MUCH PARENT INVOLVEMENT

Sam's math teacher his junior year was an excessively hard grader who had a reputation for playing favorites. Sure enough, Sam received his lowest grade of the year in math. Sam's well-intentioned mother telephoned her son's first-choice college (her alma mater) to explain what her son had been up against in that class, and why they shouldn't take the grade seriously. In response to her call, the admissions person she talked to quickly took out Sam's file—and marked it for rejection. For Sam, who was on the edge of being admitted, letting his mother call for him was a "crime" this particular admissions person could not forgive. He didn't check to find out if Sam had sanctioned or instigated what his mother had done. Doubt was enough.

Parental control of any kind, if detected, can be very damaging. This is why, in the first chapter on preparation, I stressed writing the essays over an extended period of time, to get deep into your own mind and feelings. This is different from an English assignment for which style and description and storytelling mean so much. Having read thousands of college essays, I can tell you that the best essays don't sound like they are by adults. They sound like they come from the hearts of kids. This book can teach you what's most important for the colleges to learn about you, and how to avoid lethal mistakes. You can take it from there.

When you visit admissions offices for an interview, go into the waiting area completely on your own; you will appear more independent and mature than peers who shuffle in with their parents. Also, occasionally, a parent will be asked to join an applicant's interview and may fall into the trap of "explaining" a child's goals or potential. That's fine for an eighth-grader trying to get into a selective school, but not for you. Although it's unlikely you will be put in this position, be sure to go into your interviews alone. Otherwise you risk looking too weak to stand up for yourself. That will kill your chances. The reasoning goes that overly involved parents have probably been overly involved for a long time, and the student may not be able to function without them.

Was there anything helpful that Sam could have done to keep his mother from putting herself in a no-win situation with her own alma mater? The best solution would have been for Sam to stand up for himself, perhaps by either speaking to a regional college representative on his own or by confiding in his guidance counselor. The counselor could have made clear to the college that the average grade in this math class was far below the norm, and that this particular teacher used the European method of under-grading all his students to keep them from getting overconfident. This was the truth in this case, but when a parent gets involved directly, the child looks weak and dependent.

DANGER: PREPROFESSIONAL MAJORS

Colleges do encourage you to declare an intended major, and a few prefer students who know exactly where they are headed ten years into the future. But the majority of liberal arts colleges prefer that you have an open mind. When you announce with great certainty that you intend to become a physician or a businessperson, for instance, admissions people may start to wonder why. They might see you as a bit narrow, or they might question whether you have a genuine passion for medicine or economics. They may ask, are you being pushed by your parents or by your wish for financial success?

Be prepared, therefore, to back up your professed interest with reasons of your own, or you may provoke some disrespect. (At one highly competitive college, premed applicants lacking a deep interest in the sciences are known around the admissions office as "premed weenies.") Similarly, they may wonder if plans for business school reflect a genuine intellectual passion for business administration or just ordinary materialism.

As I've suggested before, it's not that colleges don't know that people choose majors and careers hoping for security and financial success. Just the opposite: Almost *everyone* would prefer to have more money and more security rather than less. If you feel this way, and that's why you want

WHAT CAN YOU DO IF YOUR PARENT IS TRYING TOO HARD?

The line between a student's role in the admissions process and a parent's role should be clear. Just as you allow yourself to be infantilized by your parents if you allow them to do your academic work for you, you lose something of yourself if they are writing or speaking for you in the application process. If you feel that you have parents who are trying too hard, try to show them that you can do it on your own. Communicate, for parents have every right to care and to know what you're doing or not doing. If you procrastinate, they will lose confidence in you. Don't put them in that awkward position of feeling they have to take over. Your voice will be more powerful in your essays than anyone's, so take control. The colleges will be most interested in the single person who comes through to them in your essays. You are the only one who is an expert on yourself. They aren't looking for factual information, salesmanship, or dramatic creativity. They want to know if you as a person are a good fit for their school.

to be a doctor or a lawyer or a stockbroker, try to think of your other reasons, too, such as what turns you on intellectually about the field or what emotional significance it has for you. Play down the notion of personal gain.

Remember that admissions committees have many similar candidates to choose from. If two premed applicants look the same on paper, but one speaks with feeling about her interest in chemistry, physics, and biology, while the other appears just to want a good professional life or to express an immature romantic feeling about being a doctor, colleges will, every time, pick the one with a genuine interest in the sciences. If the colleges see that interest, then they believe the student's aspirations for studying medicine are coming from him—not from his parents, nor from his wish for material ease, nor from his ego. The applicant who loves the sciences, particularly these three sciences, is more likely to give the extra effort and become a better doctor. Of course colleges also look for altruism in their premeds, but telling colleges you want to go into medicine because you want to help people will not cut the mustard unless you have intellectual passion for high school courses in chemistry, physics, and biology.

DANGER: HIGH ACHIEVEMENT

Yes, you read that correctly. High achievement can put your application in danger. High grades, awards, and striking extracurricular achievements can sink your application unless you show your connection to the subjects at which you excel, and your teachers laud you for your genuine interest in their subjects. If you seem motivated by relentlessly ambitious parents or by a selfish drive for success at all costs, colleges will deny you. A lack of genuine interest in academic subjects is reason to reject a valedictorian.

REVISING THE RULE

~~Competitive colleges want high-achieving students.~~

Competitive colleges treasure high-achieving students who have a deep personal connection to the areas in which they achieve. Every good grade or impressive accomplishment raises questions you may have to answer: Whom did you excel for? What does it mean to you? What interested you in particular about the subject? And would you do it again, if you had the choice?

SPOTLIGHTING YOUR INDEPENDENT SIDE IN THE APPLICATION

Recently, I tried to encourage a senior named Russell to reduce his course load from seven classes to five. He was overburdened, his grades were suffering, and he himself admitted that two of his electives bored him. His overall GPA was at risk, and so was the personal "story" his transcript told about him.

"But what will I do with my free time?" he asked. "No one who is anyone goes to study hall." When I suggested the library, he said, "Dude, *no one goes there.*" This senior had endangered his record with a high-risk academic program only because he didn't want to stand out from the crowd. Here was a student who was overly dependent not on his parents but on his peers. He wasn't willing to "look weird," not even if it meant a lighter course load. He didn't realize that colleges like weird. Or rather, they like the independence that makes students willing to be different, ready to go it alone when it counts.

As I mentioned in the chapter on intellectual passion, the advice that "colleges like a well-rounded applicant" is misleading and dangerous. General well-roundedness can look not only like a lack of passion but also like a lack of independence. You need to make your own way. They're looking for some quirkiness, some individuality.

One student I knew decided in his senior year to skip the advanced placement courses in economics and statistics that both his school counselor and father wanted him to take, since he was thinking about being a business major in college. Instead he opted for AP art history and AP studio art. He was not an artist, but he was intrigued by how art made history come alive for him and he also wanted to try painting and drawing, which he had reluctantly discontinued in the fifth grade. As a result, he wrote some articles for the school newspaper defending arts education (which was facing budget cuts) and explaining how art provides insight into history. "Even the architecture of some periods," he wrote, "can tell you something about the spirit and philosophy of a people." He didn't actually know

---

DANGER SIGN: *Relying too much on other people's opinions*

When we're not sure what to say, many of us often fall back on the opinions of others we know and respect. When you're at a loss for words, it's easy to say, "My dad says . . ." or "My teacher says . . ." But if you hear yourself doing that a lot in an interview or an essay, it's time to reach down deep and say something of your own. Interviews are an admissions committee's best chance to find out what you really think, and not just what you've heard someone else say, or what you think you ought to say.

how this related to his long-term goals, but he felt like he was onto something, and so he stuck to his guns and took these courses. Colleges were impressed with his independent spirit, his commitment to learning, and his genuine interest.

One applicant, Becky, was asked what books she'd read that year that got her thinking. She gave an impressive-sounding answer: *Madame Bovary*, the great novel by Flaubert. Her interviewer knew the novel, too, and asked her what she'd liked about it.

"Everyone says it's one of the most important novels there is," Becky said.

The interviewer was silent.

"It's about this young woman in France," Becky went on, "who is very affected by the popular culture of her day, like the books she reads. And she has a bad marriage because she's been confused by it all."

"That was what it got you thinking about, popular culture?" the interviewer asked.

Unfortunately, it wasn't. Becky was not really thinking about how pop culture affects people's decisions. She was simply repeating the main point her English teacher had made about the book. She didn't remember reading the book all that clearly, and she hadn't actually enjoyed it. But she thought it was the kind of book you were supposed to talk about in a college interview. When pressed, she explained that her teacher had helped her to see how the story related to popular culture.

Now, I don't think the interviewer expected her to have a fluent understanding of that difficult novel. The interviewer didn't expect anything—after all, Becky had chosen to talk about the novel by herself. What concerned the interviewer was the lack of independence in her comments. "She seemed to think the point of discussing novels was to tell me whatever her teacher said," the interviewer confided to me later. "I wasn't sure if she'd even thought about it for herself."

SHOWING YOUR INDEPENDENCE
IN THE ESSAY

Some common essay questions are sucker topics that lure you to portray yourself as dependent and intellectually immature. These include:

"Describe someone you admire."

"Tell us about someone who has influenced you."

Anything about teachers, coaches, or similar figures in your life.

Let's look at an example: "I don't know what I will do without my sister when I go off to college," one young woman wrote. "How will I make it without her? She has been my rudder and my strength." What's wrong with this? While it's complimentary to the sister, it also sounds obviously exaggerated; but regardless, it exudes dependency. The writer has gone beyond saying that her sister gives her strength, to the point of implying that without her she might collapse—or worse. That's exactly the kind of dependence that makes an admissions person nervous—after all, her sister isn't coming along with her to college, is she?

When you're describing someone who's made your life better, it's easy to get carried away and make it sound like you were helpless and pitiful before that someone came along. The same can happen in descriptions of teachers. Karim, a bright but overly modest young man, wrote: "My History teacher was always willing to help me when I became confused. She patiently always took the extra time to be sure I understood. Without her insight, I would have been lost and totally bored. She pulled me through her course." And, as if that didn't make Karim seem overly dependent already, he hanged

---

STEPS TO SUCCESS

Show colleges your independent side, the part of you that will make the best possible use of the freedom college offers.

- Come out from behind the opinions of your teachers, your parents, or your friends and show your own independent thoughts and values.
- Be prepared to explain your own personal reasons for preferring one school or course of study over another.
- If you're expressing praise or admiration for someone else, don't feel you have to lower yourself in comparison.

---

himself by adding, "I could never think on my own at the level Mrs. B took me."

This was a young man who had written some good history papers in which he demonstrated the ability to reason independently, someone who, on his own, read Will Durant, the philosophically oriented historian. He had even read three of Dumas Malone's six volumes on Thomas Jefferson. Karim was a credible history buff who completely misrepresented himself. The impression he created was of a student just barely starting to "get" history. "His teacher may have shown him how to get there with help," his interviewer told me, "but we have plenty of applicants who can get there on their own."

CHAPTER EIGHT

FATAL MISTAKE #8

Going Negative

Beware this error if . . .

—*You're known to be highly critical*

—*You can seem withdrawn or slow to warm up to people*

—*You're uncomfortable showing enthusiasm or passion—
you prefer to be "cool."*

*. . . but no matter who you are, you should read the next two
pages!*

A talented writer and passionate reader, Barbara was asked a seemingly ideal question for such a good student at the start of her first interview: "What's your favorite subject in school?"

"Well . . ." she said, "I don't like math. . . . I don't really like physics and chemistry either. . . . [Long pause] . . . I guess I don't mind biology or history. . . . [Another pause] . . ."

What was going wrong? The interviewer had asked about her favorite subject, so why was she listing all the classes she *didn't* like?

For a lot of applicants, especially when they feel the added pressure of responding formally to an interview or essay question, it's hard to talk positively about themselves and what they love. It can feel . . . awkward. Childish. Embarrassing. Some applicants may feel uncool gushing about themselves or their studies. Others may just take a while to warm up. There are many reasons, but they all share one result: The applicants miss their chance to talk about what they like, the interests they care about, and all the positive aspects of themselves as applicants and as people. Instead, they go negative.

Barbara did recover later on by showing her enthusiasm for literature and philosophy, but her first remarks were hard to overcome. First impressions are the strongest; and as her interviewer told me later, "It seems Barbara dislikes many of her classes." Her real enthusiasm and insight got lost, and when I called to follow up, the feedback from the admissions office was clear: "Too negative."

Why is it so important to show your positive side? Imagine you are an admissions person. You care about your school. You want the students to be happy and productive. And what makes people more happy and productive than to be around upbeat, excited, motivated, enthusiastic peers? So that's what you're looking for: positive students. Applicants need to demonstrate their positive side in whatever ways they can.

There's another reason negativity matters. Imagine again that you are an admissions person. It's your job. You're not just a representative of the school, you're also a regular person who gets up and goes in to work and talks to various college applicants, positive, negative, and all sorts in between. Whom would you rather talk to? Positive feeling and positive energy are contagious. They rub off on everyone.

"SPARE ME"

Maybe you don't like the sound of this. Maybe all this talk about positive feeling is making you feel . . . annoyed. Snide. Negative. One student said to me, "Oh, great. Not only do these interviewers have all the power, but now we're supposed to suck up to them too?"

I understand that it can make you feel helpless and possibly frightened to be interviewed by some strange overdressed older person, so it might surprise you to hear that admissions people also feel some nervousness. For every student they recommend for acceptance, there are several they have to reject. That may be the worst part of the job: They have to disappoint people for a living. And if that were your job, wouldn't you want to feel really good about the candidates you did accept? Wouldn't you want to feel they were positive, inspiring people?

I'm definitely not suggesting that when you go to your interview you "suck up"—fake enthusiasm isn't just wrong, it's also rarely convincing and often depressing. But if you have two sides, if you're capable of any honest positive feeling, then remember that a college application is a place to show how things look to you when the glass looks half full. You don't have to do this every moment of your life, but for the purpose of your application, it's best to show your positive side.

WHAT'S SO HARD ABOUT STAYING POSITIVE?

Maybe this doesn't sound so hard. Yet I see so many applicants, even those who have positive feelings about the colleges they want to attend and the high school from which they're graduating, who come across as negative. Many don't even realize the impression they create. In part that's because there are so many reasons applicants can appear to be negative. Read through this list, and consider whether any of these might apply to you.

- *You're too cool to gush*. Negativity, cynicism, and keeping a distance may be cool among your friends. Often the style is not to admit you care about your school life, your teachers, even your future plans. One college student I knew was an example. When I saw him near the end of his senior year, I asked, "What are you going to do after you graduate?" He answered, "I'll probably go see a movie." It was a clever response, and it let me know that he didn't want to be quizzed about his future plans. Still, that approach is dangerous in an interview or essay, or in talking with the teachers or counselors who may write about you. If you pretend you don't care, you may be mistaken for someone who really doesn't care. What's cool among your peers may kill you with admissions people.

- *You're in a negative mood that day.* One applicant started his personal essay this way: "Most days for me are not significant. They are routine, endless exercises that usually start off at 6:00 A.M., a time which I am never happy to see." Now, we all know what it feels like to be unhappy when the alarm sounds. And maybe that was the mood this writer was in when he wrote these lines. But when you put a passing mood into an essay, it starts to seem like the way you see your entire life. On paper, that passing mood seems to suggest something disturbing about your character: that you lack the emotional strength for an intense experience like college, or that you give up easily, spoiling your own chances for success.

  Can admissions people know these things are true about you? No, of course not. The most they would have is a concern, a worry. But they have many applicants to choose from, so they may decide, why take the risk? Why not pick another student who doesn't seem to have a viewpoint so bleak that he or she can't flourish in the challenges of college life?

- *You just feel uncomfortable.* Some people feel squeamish about sharing their good feelings and asserting their accomplishments. They are naturally modest, and they are more

---

INTERVIEW FIRST AID

What if you don't know whether you come off as negative?

If you're not sure whether you have a tendency to seem negative to adults, give this list to an adult you trust, and let her help you decide if any of these describe you.

comfortable voicing criticisms than praise or enthusiasm. I respect that, but I've noticed that when something else adds to their discomfort—pressure to impress an interviewer, say—they often start to exaggerate their modesty, until they seem actively apologetic or as if they don't like themselves. So even to those people I say: Negativity tends to snowball. Don't let your discomfort make you argue against your own promise.

And here's something I've noticed. For many applicants, when I tell them that they're not *supposed* to be negative, it comes as a relief. It makes them more comfortable and lets them speak more easily about themselves, and the negativity fades.

UNMAKING THE MISTAKE: THE CURE FOR NEGATIVITY

You're asked a question, whether in person or on paper, and a negative answer comes to your mind. What do you do? You let whatever comes up come up in your mind—negative, positive, or in between. Wait a moment, then think of a few answers. Consider your options and then pick something positive to say. Then say something else that is positive. Pause in between if you need to. *Say everything positive about the question that you can think of.* Say nothing negative until you're out of positives. Then pick one negative. Now you're starting to get the balance right.

Remember Barbara, who couldn't manage to tell her interviewer anything about the classes that she really did like? This is the conversation I had with Barbara after her interview bogged down in negativity. She'd learned she had been rejected for early admission, and now we were practicing for her next set of interviews.

"Okay. Let's try it again," I said. "What's your favorite subject in school?"

"Well . . . I don't know about *favorite* . . ."

"You don't?" I asked.

"Doesn't it sound kind of babyish? Hey, little girl, what's your favorite subject in school?"

"Maybe it does. But they really do want to know."

"And I'm not telling them," she said.

"Not yet."

"I'm still being negative?"

"Don't you hear it?"

"Okay, okay," she said. "Ask me again."

"So, what's your favorite subject in school?"

"My favorite subject is English."

"And why is that?"

"I like novels."

"Yes? What do you like about them?"

"I like what you can learn about the world when you read them."

"Yes?"

"It's like they open up these windows onto other places and times, and you can go there. Instant travel. In fact it's better than going to the real places."

"Really? How is it better?"

"It's better in a way, because you get to go into people's lives and hear what they say when they're in private—even their thoughts. You have more access. You can see how people actually live and how they're so different from each other but also the same. I'd have to live with someone for months or years to get to know them as well as I know the people in a good novel. An English class doesn't even feel like work to me." Now, *that* was a positive answer to the question! If she had started here and stayed on this track, her early-decision result would likely have been different.

DON'T OFFER A HARD SELL

But be careful. Don't get the wrong idea. I've seen applicants convince themselves that if it's good to be positive, it's better to be very positive and it's best of all to be insanely positive. They turn into ruthless salespeople, touting their positive qualities and achievements, even ones they don't actually have. Rob, for example, had good SATs and good solid grades in a credible academic program, but for him a top-tier college was a reach. When he wrote his personal statement to a college a little over his head, he went into a hard-sell mode:

> I carry the discussion in many of my classes; my SAT's are close to the 700's and I get a substantial number of A's. I believe I am regarded as one of the best editors of the school newspaper in recent years; I am a leading scorer on the varsity soccer team, and more than anyone else I have helped to raise the level of giving in our community for Oxfam. Considering how well-rounded I am, I should be considered in the top 10% of my class in overall ability and contribution to my school.

That all sounded good, and to some extent, it did match what the college was hearing about him from others. His teachers wrote that he was active in the classroom, a dependable student in a solid program, and an above-average editor of the school paper. His guidance counselor wrote that he was an effective fund-raiser for Oxfam and a courageous soccer player on a terrible team. They liked him a lot, but it would have been better if they had said the things that Rob was saying about himself. Overall, he seemed too assertive, too conscious of his own standing among his peers. Rather than selling his accomplishments so hard, he would have been better off emphasizing his academic interests and how he liked to fit into a community. With his hard-sell approach he was virtually saying, "I don't trust my school to say enough good things about me."

BUT WHAT IF YOU REALLY
ARE NEGATIVE?

There are two other reasons for negativity we need to mention:

- *You act negatively about a particular college because you are negative about that college, or about the colleges other people think you should apply to, or about college in general.* What if you don't want to work on applications and go on interviews? What if you don't want to go to college at all, or you don't care to do the extra work that might get you into a school that for you is a reach? Then your negativity is not a misrepresentation. It's what you really feel. If you can't change your mind about it, then you might do well to save yourself the effort, save your family a lot of money, and consider a less expensive school. Perhaps you could get a job and reconsider college after working for a year. It may sound radical, but especially if you're applying to expensive colleges, why not save the money until you feel excited and ready? Most kids who take a year or two off discover why they want to go back to academics, and the colleges welcome their being older. If you're motivated, you'll be able to make up for lost time, and if you're not, you might find something that suits you better. There are many American success stories with no chapter about college.

- *You act negatively because something truly terrible has happened.* What if you've had a death in your family or a brutal divorce or some other profoundly negative event in your life? Then negativity isn't a tendency to guard against, it's a natural reaction to your personal history. If that's your situation, turn to Chapter Twelve, on dealing with rough times.

Staying Positive in the Interview

Be prepared for the common question "What is your greatest weakness?" It's dangerous, because with this question there isn't just a *risk* that you'll go negative, it's a requirement. Once you start, there is a tendency for negatives to snowball, calling up more and more dark feelings (disappointment, frustration, anger) until you seem to disappear into the black hole of your own negativity.

One young woman said that her biggest weakness was her shyness. She started describing how she would withdraw from large groups, and how many bad memories she had of embarrassing situations and missed opportunities. As she spoke, she lost her sense of humor. Her mood turned glum. She seemed consumed by her bad memories and unable to stop thinking about them. The black hole of negativity had claimed another victim.

To keep away from its dangerous gravity, I suggest first of all that applicants pick out a flaw or setback in advance, with one—just one—specific example of how it's been a problem. That way you can give a good specific answer and then move on before the emotions start to snowball. Does this mean that your interviewer won't hear the whole story? Yes, it does. But remember where you are. A college interview is not a place for full confessions, or for therapeutic extremes of honesty. Nor is it like talking to a friend. Now, don't get me wrong. If you're lucky, you'll like your interviewer. In rare cases, the interviewer might go on to become a mentor and maybe one day even a friend. But that day is far off. For now, the interviewer is doing his or her job, which is to weed out many applicants and recommend a few. If you feel the need for a sympathetic ear, this isn't the place. Say enough that your interviewer understands the weakness you mean, and then move on.

But move on where? To the second half of the question, the unspoken half. When interviewers ask you about your flaws, they're hoping to hear about more than just flaws. It's common to have weaknesses. Everyone has them. What's uncommon is to find someone who sees them clearly and handles them well. So they want to hear about how clearly you see yourself and how you handle what you see. If they ask you about your least favorite subject, they're hoping to hear how you persevered in the face of a requirement you didn't love. It's like that old expression you may have heard about what to do when life gives you lemons. When interviewers invite you to talk about bad experiences, they want to hear honestly about the lemons in your life, yes; but what they really want is your recipe for lemonade.

One approach to this "second half of the question" is to describe how you've paid special attention to what has been difficult for you, given it extra time, and, as a result, found it interesting and valuable. One student I knew had such trouble with public speaking that she couldn't speak in classes of more than about thirty. She gave that weakness some special attention, and she was able to say this: "I'm nervous in front of large groups, but I'm taking Public Speaking for People Who Hate It. That's a course at our community college, and it's helped." If you've struggled with a particular course and your grade has improved, say so. If your grade hasn't improved, but you feel a change on the inside, you can say that too. One student I knew said, "I am still not getting a great grade, but in my own mind, I am getting an A out of the course." He went on to explain why—he found this subject extremely interesting, and his interviewer was convinced of his sincerity.

What if you've done nothing at all about your weakness? Then pick another weakness to describe. Everyone has some that she's worked on and some that she hasn't. Show that you have the maturity to pick one you've started to address; give a short objective description of the trouble you've had, and then soar into what you are doing about it and what you feel good about.

Staying Positive in the Essay

Here are two more common questions that can lure you into deadly negativity:

- *Explore an experience that changed you.* Here the risk is that in order to have a really dazzling "after" picture, showing how the experience made you stronger, you'll create such a dismal "before" picture that the bad picture will steal the show, and what your reader will remember is the mess you say you used to be. As with describing a weakness, keep the description of the "old you" to an efficient minimum, and spend most of your time on the experience that changed you and all the good ways you changed.

- *Describe a typical day.* There are two risks here. The first is that you'll get started on the negatives—the responsibilities you wish you didn't have, the people you don't like, a long laundry list of complaints about teachers who misunderstand and classmates who cheat and all the ugliness and hypocrisy in the world, everywhere, piling up, suffocating you—arggh!— until the negativity snowball rolls away with you. The second risk is that you'll slip into escapism, talking about how much you love to relax and veg out and watch TV and sleep. There's nothing wrong with any of those, but what the schools want to know, I think, is how you put your days together and what you get out of them. Pick a day with substance, and then show what interests you and how you connect with other people: the classes and activities you look forward to, the little things that you find exhilarating and interesting, the places that are important, whatever makes your day worthwhile.

THE DANGER IN A SINGLE
NEGATIVE WORD

Sometimes just one word or phrase can put a gloomy picture in a reader's mind. Remember that admissions people may be evaluating twenty or more applications in a night. Sometimes a single image, if it's vivid enough, or even one single, powerful, damaging word, can become the lasting impression the reader takes away. Simply based on your word choice, college admissions readers may think they intuit character flaws: a lack of confidence, a tendency toward aggression, emotional instability, and so on.

Here is one applicant describing his disappointment with a picture of himself in the local paper. In the photograph he was performing stand-up comedy:

> The newspaper hardly acknowledged me except to include my name at the bottom of the list of participants. I had felt a great connection with the audience, which consistently laughed at my jokes. The photographer also got me at an uncomplimentary angle. My face was contorted and my mother expressed surprise that I looked so awkward and unconfident. Also, my body took on a paunchy look, so I got concerned about what my friends at school would think, especially my girlfriend.

In this case, the description is really too good for the purpose it serves in the essay, too memorably negative. The student got caught up in his penchant for description. Later in the essay, he describes how successful that event had been for him, as his own original use of political satire was a hit. But by sharing his feelings about the painfully awkward newspaper picture, he emphasized his concerns about his image among his peers. And he risked having that image linger on in the reader's mind and leaving an overall negative impression. So I encourage you to minimize negative descriptions and to leave out words that might overshadow an otherwise strong essay. Unless they are essential to the point you are making, remove pejorative words and images that describe you as:

Humiliated

Depressed

Bored

STEPS TO SUCCESS

Whether you are naturally a positive person, a negative person, or somewhere in between, show colleges that you have the *ability* to be positive.

How?

- Get help from others to determine if you are prone to "go negative."
- Practice starting with the positive things you believe and then adding in just a little negative for balance.
- Be true to yourself, but let the positive side of yourself come first.

Angry

Shy

Inhibited

Overwhelmed

Anxious

Frightened

Frustrated

Defeated

Stressed

Not all of life is positive, and not every situation requires a positive response. But if you can keep unnecessary and accidental negatives out of your application, then colleges get the best possible chance to respond to *you* positively.

CHAPTER NINE

FATAL MISTAKE #9

Exclusivity

Beware this error if . . .

   —You know your crowd and you tend to stick with it

Two male athletes from the same high school came for on-campus interviews on the same day. The first had higher test scores and a higher grade point average than the second. As athletes, the appeal they held for this college's coaches was about the same.

"Tell me about yourself," the interviewer asked the first athlete.

"I mostly hang with other athletes," he said. "We just kind of stick together. You know, we sit together in class, and we go out together after practice or on the weekends. You know how it is."

Later the interviewer asked if he had any questions about the school. "Do athletes enjoy high status on campus?" he asked. "Do your students come to the games?"

The second athlete met with the same interviewer. He asked, "Are athletes accepted here, or are they seen as most likely less intelligent? I'd like to make some friends who aren't athletes. Is it hard, do you think?"

The second athlete, the one with the lower scores, was admitted.

The first athlete was not. Why? Because American colleges are experiments in cultural diversity. They bring together students from the broadest possible range of backgrounds and from around the world, to give them the opportunity to learn from each other. This prepares them for a future in an increasingly global world. But the experiment can't get started unless the students do more together than sit side by side in lecture halls. The second athlete wanted to make friends with students who were not necessarily athletes; he wanted to be part of the community as a whole. This made him the more desirable candidate of the two.

Recently, I visited a college that was proud of the breadth of its student population. Not only did it draw students from virtually every state but from dozens of countries around the world. However, as I walked through the campus I noticed something strange. I saw people in pairs and in small groups, and they all seemed to match. There were Asian kids talking to Asian kids, African kids talking to African kids, and everywhere I looked there seemed to be like people spending time with like people. The school was drawing an international student body, all right, but it wasn't creating an international community. As far as Americans actually sharing in the mix of international perspectives, the foreign students might as well have stayed at home. Why were there no Americans among them? I wondered. Didn't the Americans on campus see the opportunities, personal as well as intellectual, to make friends from other countries? Didn't they realize how much they might grow from these friendships? And on a less selfish note, couldn't they imagine how lonely it must be for foreign peers who felt cut off from most of their classmates?

That school faced a strong challenge in helping to bring students from different places together, but every school faces this dilemma to some degree. For this reason, colleges hope you'll be a "bridge builder," an informal cultural ambassador who can tolerate unfamiliarity and difference, become part of the whole community, and inspire others to do the same. Otherwise, everyone misses out, and everyone gets a lesser education.

I JUST WANT TO FEEL COMFORTABLE

Now, I know that we all have times we tend to stick with familiar-seeming people who make us feel safe and at home. No school expects anyone to give up the comfort of being around whatever sort of people help you feel like you belong. What they do hope, though, is that you will also grab opportunities to reach out of your "comfort zone" and make unexpected connections.

How? Some high school students do this in a public way, for example, by joining or even starting an organization that helps make connections among people on campus or that includes peers from other towns, or between students and the people in their communities, whether these communities are the surrounding town or the support staff of the college. Just getting a job where you work with people who are different from the ones with whom you normally hang around can go a long way toward showing that you are not limited to one exclusive group. I also knew a group of friends who organized an after-school sports program in a neighborhood that was racially mixed. Kids in the program started talking openly with each other about race, which led to the establishment of regular forums on racial issues, sponsored by the community.

Other high school students reach out in more private ways. They make personal connections with people they meet in their dorms or neighborhoods or classrooms. It's easy to fall into the habit of only talking to people in your usual groups, but it's not so hard to start talking to others as well.

Whether you take a public approach or a more private one, in the eyes of the colleges both approaches count. But if you only seem to cling to those just like you, then as far as the colleges are concerned you are an obstacle to the community they're trying to build.

MAKING A CONNECTION

A good first step is to imagine similarities and common ground you may have with people who seem very different. In other words, the first step to overcoming the tendency to be exclusive that we all share is to develop your social sensitivity, as I said in Chapter Six. But avoiding this deadly mistake takes more than sensitivity. Just as you can become an intellectual leader by turning your own private intellectual passion outward to benefit the whole community, you can become a bridge builder by turning your social sensitivity outward to act on the opportunities that you sense. In fact, if you feel you are weak in moral imagination, or the ability to imagine yourself in someone else's shoes, one of the best things you can do is to start talking to people unlike yourself and listen to what they have to say. The more you build bridges and keep an open mind, the more your ability to be inclusive and supportive of others will grow without any sort of special study.

I remember a very difficult night at a boarding school where I taught. A female teacher had been assaulted on campus. She had been tied up and raped. That evening, in response to this awful news, fifty or sixty students gathered in one of the dorm common areas to be with each other. As they sat on couches and on the floor, some of the young women present shared their feelings. They described feeling haunted by what they'd heard the teacher had gone through. They shared how profoundly hurt, degraded, and angry they felt.

At first, in stark contrast, the male students showed only mild sympathy. They could not fully understand the depth of their female friends' devastation. One young man pointed out that the teacher had not been killed or maimed. He said, "I just wish everybody would chill out."

Some of the female students got angry. Didn't he understand how this affected all of the women at the school? they wanted to know. "What is the matter with the guys?" a young woman asked. "Don't you have any compassion?" The room grew tense as the other boys in the room identified with their fellow male who had spoken out.

Finally, one of the young men spoke.

"You know," he said, "maybe I don't understand. Maybe it's because I'm a guy and maybe it's not, I don't really know. But I do know that what happened to [the teacher] shouldn't happen to anyone, and if I don't understand it all, then I want to stay here and listen and try to understand a little more. But the important thing I think is that all the guys here care about your feelings. And we are sorry, even if we don't understand."

I admired that student very much for what he said. Many of the male students had been feeling an exclusivity impulse, willing to only relate to their own male feelings. But now as the meeting went on, they began to show compassion for the women present, who were visibly suffering. They overcame traditional masculine logic and became comforters. In this way, despite the terrible assault, the students were able to build bridges across their differences and stand together at a difficult time.

REVISING THE RULE

~~Travel to foreign countries proves you are a culturally sophisticated, "inclusive" applicant.~~

Travel shows the *potential* for building bridges, but you still have to show the schools what connections you made with people you met—and what you learned from those connections. You can expect some skepticism (and some follow-up questions in interviews) if all you do is list the countries you may have visited.

WHERE CAN YOU BUILD BRIDGES?

You can build bridges on athletic teams, in school organizations, and among your student body as a whole. You might do it in surrounding communities—across town, not just across the world. Bridge-building is also an essential part of many extracurriculars. (If you play on a sports team where your teammates are from different racial or economic backgrounds, or volunteer to tutor a kid from a disadvantaged part of your area, or attend an interfaith conference as a representative of your place of worship, these are opportunities to show that you've chosen to put yourself in situations where you had no choice but to try to make connections with people unlike you. Of course, it's still up to you to make clear in your applications how you learned from these experiences, and how much of a difference they have really made in your life.

As these examples show, you don't need to go to exotic locales to find different varieties of people and the opportunity to build bridges among them. There are opportunities to build bridges even in your own high school or neighborhood. The chance might come between athletes and scholars, artists and scientists, the book-smart and the street-smart, liberals and conservatives, male and female, rich and poor. You might find it among people of a different race or religion or age, among city kids and suburban kids and kids from the country. And wherever you find these opportunities, colleges are hoping not just that you encounter people unlike yourself, but that you show the courage to interact with them and listen to them, and then the willingness to try to bond with them. Then you will be expected to reflect on the experience. It's that combination of social courage and willingness to reflect that admissions people look for in your application, your interviews, and your essays.

Building Bridges in the Application

Some applicants assume that the key to demonstrating their ability to learn from a broad range of people is to show where they have traveled. Some who think this way are misled, often by adults, even parents, who in their time might have gotten kudos from colleges for being "well-traveled." Foreign places are filled with foreign people and cultures, of course, so these students spotlight the countries they have visited on their brag sheets. However, those who take this approach may not realize that plane tickets and stamps on a passport are no guarantee, in colleges' eyes, that you actually spoke to anyone for longer than it took to order dinner.

Building Bridges in the Interview

One of our students listed in her application all the countries in Europe she'd been fortunate enough to visit the summer after her junior year in high school. An interviewer asked her, "What do you think that means, that you got to visit many countries?"

"It's an important cultural experience!" she answered. She went on to list some of her visits to famous museums, theaters, cathedrals, and castles. "It was all really cultural," she said. She kept using the word *cultural*. She used it until it sounded completely empty of meaning. When asked what she had learned from these "cultural" experiences, she could not describe anything about the nature of the people she'd met, or, more importantly, about their ways of seeing the world. The interviewer said afterward, "She could list the countries she'd visited and the sights she'd seen, but her mind never went anywhere new." Admissions people are most interested to know if you will let yourself take in new points of view and learn from them. This student's experience had been enjoyable, but apparently it hadn't gone any deeper, prompting her to think or feel anything she hadn't thought or felt before.

In contrast, another student, Marya, also went abroad, where she stayed in a hotel run by nuns. One morning she saw a young nun sitting in a small courtyard drinking her coffee. The nun looked a lot like her best friend, which gave Marya a little extra confidence to sit down next to her and try to have a conversation. It happened that the nun knew some English, and the two of them fumbled through two languages, with a lot of hand gestures and laughter, talking about the different choices they were making in their lives, and why they were making them. When Marya came home she told me, "I'll never think of nuns in the same way again." She'd made a connection and it had touched her. In time it changed her thinking. Although agnostic, she came back with considerably more respect for people in religious orders. That's what colleges are hoping to see.

AN INTERVIEW IS A CHANCE TO BUILD A BRIDGE

There is really no place more perfect for showing off your bridge-building skills than the college interview itself. Your interviewer will be older than you and most likely will have perspectives different from yours. Things that may seem everyday to you may be mysterious or confusing to him or her. And so interviewers watch to see what you will do when you have to talk to a stranger who is, in a sense, foreign. How do you handle it?

One applicant I know, Charlene, described herself this way: "I'm totally into Gwen Stefani. I love practically every album she's ever done. And it's not just that—she's my role model, really. Not that I'm a singer or a dancer or a fashion designer, at least not yet, but just the whole way she's built her career. I admire that so much."

The interviewer looked perplexed. "I'm sorry," he said. "I don't know this Stefani. It's not that I'm not a music fan, mind you. I just heard Bobby Short last week at the Carlisle Club. Do you know him?"

Charlene shook her head no.

"Well," said the interviewer, "I sit with young people like yourself, and they tell me these things like, 'I'm all about Green Day.' 'I'm into 50 Cent.' But I don't even know if 50 Cent is the name of an ensemble or a solo artist. What am I supposed to say?"

Charlene didn't get embarrassed, and she didn't get disappointed or impatient. Instead, she started to describe what she thought these different musicians represented to people her age, in terms of shared values. And her interviewer was impressed—not with her musical knowledge, which he had no way to judge, but with the sensitive way she acknowledged the gap between his musical background and hers, and the way she was able to bridge that gap by imagining what it would be like not to know, and to need help understanding. She never did convince him to download a Gwen Stefani album, but he still recommended Charlene for admission.

DO YOU THINK BEYOND YOUR CLIQUE?

Some applicants appear cliquey and exclusive in the questions they ask their interviewers. They ask, "Do you have a strong Greek system here?" Or, like the athlete at the start of this chapter: "Do athletes [like me] enjoy high status?" Questions like these may make interviewers wonder if the applicant will reach beyond the narrow group he hopes to join. I encourage students to pose questions that also acknowledge the other students on campus. Having been briefed on the Greek system, some have asked, "How do students who aren't in fraternities and sororities socialize here?" You might even go further, asking, "Does the faculty think the Greek system is good for the school community?"

Maybe this seems artificial. Is it a good idea to push yourself to ask some questions like these that are broader in their social view? Actually, the habit of thinking beyond your own needs to the needs of those who may be excluded by current social realities can lead to good things no matter why you start. Of course, if you don't care, then it's no good to ask such questions. They may lead to a conversation in which you'll only appear bored or self-absorbed. But if you feel some interest in building bridges, then it's worth letting an interviewer see that interest in action.

Building Bridges in the Essay

Some colleges ask direct questions on the application about exclusivity. Tufts University has asked applicants to write about experiences that have prepared them for the ethnic, international, and socioeconomic diversity they will find at the school. They know that no sane applicant is going to write, "I'm cliquey and afraid of people who aren't just like me." So usually colleges come at it indirectly. It seems to me that there are two kinds of essays intended to draw out the tendency to exclude.

The first is the essay that asks for a description of an ideal roommate, or for a letter to a hypothetical roommate. I believe these are designed in part to flush out closed attitudes. I've seen many an essay on this question that manifests the writer's fears about having to live with someone from a different social background. One student of mine actually wrote the following as the opening of his hypothetical letter:

Dear Potential Roommate:

After four years of boarding school, I've found that social diversity is great for the school community as a whole, especially for classroom discussion. But for a roommate, I think it's important to be with a totally compatible person. I come from a fairly formal family. I was a regular escort at debutante balls, so I'm not a T-shirt person with my baseball hat on backwards. I hope to pledge my father's fraternity, as I'll be third generation. I'm also a connoisseur of good wines (off campus, of course) and women are my weakness. So I hope you don't mind if I entertain in the room once in a while. On the other hand, I am a serious student who reads a lot, so I also like the room to be quiet during times when we aren't partying or talking philosophy. But do tell me about yourself, and please be candid about whether or not you think we might be a good fit.

The second kind of dangerous essay is one we've touched on already: any essay that shows how you approach your interactions and experiences with people unlike you whom you don't know. Admissions readers want to know if applicants make an attempt to understand the people they meet outside their own small circle of friends. I am repeating this idea in this section on the essay, because it is critical to remember. Any city or town offers the chance to meet a wide range of people. It may be easier to have a true cultural experience by getting to know your hometown better, rather than flying off to stay in hotels and see famous sights. It does not have to be a spectacular experience or event. By working at a McDonald's or bagging groceries, you interact with a variety of people to whom you have to reach out if you are to begin to understand and to connect with them.

Here are some questions likely to be on the mind of an admissions person reading an essay in which you describe experiences of new places (near or far) and encounters with people you didn't know before:

What sort of relationships did you form?

If you didn't form relationships, then what did you observe by watching another country's television and reading its newspapers?

Did you notice how its educational system differs from ours?

What surprised or interested you about what you found?

If you went to museums or sampled other cultural experiences, what in them got you thinking?

The important thing is to show that you can connect with different sorts of people and on top of that to reflect on what you discover with them.

Bill wrote about spending a summer in a foreign country. He stayed with a well-off family who had three other guests, two from Asia and one from Europe. Bill described how each of the guests responded differently to living in a new language and culture, and how even something as simple as choosing a hot drink to sip at breakfast could set off cultural confusion: The family assumed that each visitor would announce his or her preference and stick with it, while the visitors were hoping to try out different drinks. The confusion that resulted allowed Bill to describe a funny and heartwarming series of light misunderstandings. Still, at the end of his essay, he just left us there with an entertaining memory. He portrayed himself as amused, but he didn't talk about what he'd learned about the thoughts of people in this foreign place, or how he'd been changed by the experience.

When I asked him what had happened to him that was significant, he said, "Just the obvious, really. We had fun together, and I took classes at their school, and it was pretty cool. Then I came home."

I explained that this wasn't enough. It was fun to read about his funny experiences, but I still didn't know what difference the experiences had made to him. What changed in his perspective as a result of this time away?

In his next revision, he wrote:

I became close to six people, all of different nationalities and religions. I didn't agree with any of them about everything, and I didn't disagree with any of them about everything. We saw each other every day, and we managed to like each other and sometimes have a lot of fun. Now that I'm back home, there are some that I miss and some I don't miss so much, but I wish every one of them well.

One of my teachers back home once told us that he identified with "all people, everywhere." I didn't know what he meant, then, but now I understand. I am now, myself, an international person.

STEPS TO SUCCESS

S how colleges that you are a bridge builder, able to make connections with people from different backgrounds. Remember that such situations occur both far from home and right down the street. Your descriptions of your high school experiences are a chance to show your bridge-building skills. So are your college interviews.

In the first draft of his essay, this student had alluded to warm, personal relationships with peers of another culture. That was good, but he was applying to an academic institution that would want to know how not just his feelings, but his thinking, might have been changed by confronting another culture. They want to see emotional bridge-building, but they also want to see intellectual engagement. In this student's revision, he showed that his thinking had changed. He could now imagine himself as a member of "all people, everywhere." Becoming an "international person" meant that in a global sense, he was a bridge builder.

CHAPTER TEN

FATAL MISTAKE #10

Narrow Thinking

Beware this error if . . .
   —You like to look for the one right answer to a question

One foreign student I worked with had lived all over Asia and in Europe, and he'd studied the language in every country where he'd lived. He told me he felt confident about his interviews. "Don't worry about me getting in," he said. "I can speak twelve languages. They'll love me!" He made a point of showing his interviewers how he could translate parts of their conversation from one language to another.

What happened? He didn't get the response he expected. His interviewers acknowledged that he had an unusual skill, even an impressive one, but to them it was only that, one narrow skill. "Maybe he can speak twelve languages," his first-choice college told me. "But can he think in one?"

Colleges are looking not for narrow skills but for broad thinking. What is the difference? I'll explain with another example. An applicant I worked with was asked by an interviewer to describe the kind of student he was. "Prepared," he said. "I prepare for every class. When the teacher calls on me, I want to be right."

Were his listeners impressed? On the one hand, yes, because a prepared student is much more useful in class than an unprepared one. But on the other hand, his attitude raised concerns. So many of the questions asked in college don't have one single right answer, and if you come at them narrowly, looking for that one correct box to check, you may miss the most important parts. Most students recognize that this is true for a humanities class, such as a class in reading literature, where the work requires interpretation, not just calculation. But it's also true in the sciences, where college-level work requires not only that you know your facts, but that you try out different hypotheses, and can recognize that many of the most interesting questions are those that no one hypothesis can answer. For example, why does one person get cancer while his brother, who is genetically similar and lives in the same house, does not? Why does one country flourish while another is conquered? Even in math, when you get to a high enough level, there is no longer necessarily one correct answer. Instead, mathematicians offer competing "proofs" that may be judged based on how "elegant" and even how "beautiful" they are.

College work requires a broader perspective, at least part of the time, and so colleges are looking for students whose approach to learning is not limited just to building narrow skills or looking for the single correct answer. Yes, they want students who can think precisely and follow accepted procedures, but of those students they want the ones who can also think broadly enough to try out different possibilities—students who can explore for a while before they have to arrive somewhere certain. As Bill Fitzsimmons, director of admissions at Harvard, once said, "We want kids who are comfortable with ambiguity."

Narrow questions have a right answer, and the interest in asking them is to get to that answer as quickly and correctly as possible. Broad questions are more like taking the scenic route: You don't know where you're going, exactly, but you'll never get there if you aren't willing to explore and to think on your feet. For these reasons, colleges aren't so impressed if you can say something familiar in twelve different ways. They want to know if you can think up one interesting thing to say that's all your own.

Let me give you an example of the kind of broad thinking colleges look for. I remember when some friends and I saw the movie *Dead Man Walking*. In the movie, Sean Penn plays a cruel and vicious murderer who is on death row. He shows a glimmer of his humanity to a nun, played by Susan Sarandon. The movie touches on a theme that sometimes surfaces in literature: a totally despicable protagonist who, in the end, does one good thing, testing readers to see if they can still feel for that person. The same theme occurs in *Tsotsi*, an Academy Award–winning foreign-language film about an African boy who commits a string of violent crimes. He shoots and paralyzes the mother of a baby, whom he accidentally steals by taking her car. This monster of a boy, in the end, sacrifices himself to return the baby.

Upon leaving the theater after *Dead Man Walking,* I said to an old acquaintance, the CEO of a major company, "I wonder if I could be like this nun and see any amount of goodness or humanity in a brutal murderer. Could I care about him?"

"What's the point?" he answered condescendingly.

I knew what he meant. My own first reaction was that Sean Penn's character was just a cold-blooded killer and deserved no acknowledgment as a fellow human being whatsover. He was evil. Why look any deeper? I also thought this good nun was a little extreme. But considered more broadly, there was an opportunity there for some interesting thinking. Although it was enough for me to know that Sean Penn's character had committed a horrific crime, Susan Sarandon's character challenged me to think: Was he entirely evil? Or could there be a part of even an evil person that was also good? These might sound like overly objective, purely philosophical questions, but to this idealistic nun, they were important questions: He still had a soul, and he deserved to be considered a full human being, not just the emblem of his heinous act. I would not have expected that CEO or anyone else to feel sympathy for the murderer, but it was disappointing to me that he wouldn't even try to think about it.

To him, such thinking, philosophical as it may be, might be dangerous and lead to very practical questions: What, for instance, do we see as the purpose of prison or of capital punishment? What kinds of prisons should we build and how should the prisoners be treated? What does this mean to us, as Americans who support these prisons with our tax dollars?

And so on. Sometimes, even questions without any immediate practical "point" lead to important and useful thoughts. Broad thinking, then, is the willingness to follow such meandering roads to find out where they might take you. If you are willing to extend your interest and your sense of caring to a wider group of people and situations, even opening your thoughts to include people who commit evil acts, as in this case, you show a willingness to be challenged, a potential for intellectual openness that colleges look for in their applicants.

Even so, you might be feeling right now like the CEO whom I knew casually: What's the point of all of this discussion of narrow and broad thinking? Why does it matter so much? The answers go all the way back to the reasons that colleges exist, and the meaning they hold for the people who run them. To you, "college" might mean personal freedom, intellectual adventure, career development, or a chance to pursue a favorite extracurricular activity. But from the point of view of admissions people, administrators, and professors, colleges are first of all institutions of higher learning, sites of careful and skillful teaching and research, places where thinking gets done. It is crucial to them that their students possess and use their ability to think and think broadly. Signs of narrow, inflexible, and ungenerous thought suggest that, no matter how good an applicant looks on paper, he or she might not actually be a good candidate for an intellectually oriented college community. So from their point of view, broad and open thinking is the essential kind of thinking that liberal arts colleges exist to support and develop. Without it, not only is your application as good as dead— their school's reason for existing dies, too.

Of course they don't expect you to have done the learning already, but you need to show your potential. And they look for signs of that potential in your application and your interview—or for signs of its deadly absence—in practical ways. Let's consider some danger signs in detail.

A SIMPLISTIC VIEW OF THE WORLD

I've already explained how showing off narrow skills or expecting always to find a right answer can suggest to schools that you have a simplistic view of college learning. Another danger sign is the use of absolute terms, which suggests that you may see the world as a simple and certain place, easy to understand and to categorize. One student of mine wrote, in an essay about climbing a mountain, "When I got to the top of that jagged mountain peak, and looked down upon the great plains of Oregon, I knew I could do ANYTHING." Now, I think most readers understood what he was saying. He'd felt a strong emotion. He'd climbed a mountain and it made him feel powerful. But that's not what he wrote. He wrote that he could do "anything," but let's be honest. Could he fly off that mountain peak and live? Could he cure AIDS before the next victim died? Could he win a round of *American Idol*?

Let me say that I do know what that kid meant. I've also reached the top of a mountain and felt powerful. And I'd bet that everyone has had experiences like that, and felt great. The trouble is not with the experience, but with the unthoughtful way it's described. The word *anything* is an absolute, and if you use such words when they don't apply, you either sound as if you have a narrow, naïve view of the world, or as if you're not really paying attention. Admissions people may not even be sure which it is—maybe you can't think broadly, or maybe you're just not bothering to try—but either way they're hoping to see something else.

Most situations and rules, after all, have exceptions. Other possibilities almost always exist, and this is why absolute terms tend to sound ridiculous. I remember one student athlete who wrote about how he made a terrific physical comeback after getting sidelined by an injury. "I worked out and lifted weights for hours every day, but I didn't do it for myself," he wrote. "I did it only for my team." That's a nice sentiment, and of course, he did sacrifice part of himself for the team, but it would have been more mature to acknowledge his selfish interest in being healthy and getting to play. One reader responded with: "Only for the team? Really? He is a little lacking in self-awareness." Another said, "What about honesty?" Now they were imagining serious character flaws (dishonesty, self-deception) in the student, based on one word in his essay—*only*. But all of this could have been avoided if he'd shown a capacity for more intellectual depth.

Dangerous, absolutist words include:

never

always

everyone

only

nobody

Am I saying never to use an absolute word? Well, no. There are situations when these words are the only way to say what you mean. I'm suggesting that when you notice these words appearing on your computer screen, or coming out of your mouth, you stop and ask yourself, Do I really mean what I'm saying? Or did I get stuck in narrow thinking?

One student of mine wrote, "I could never trust anyone again in any circumstance if I knew that person cheated on an exam." I asked him, "Really? *Never*, not even ten, thirty, or fifty years later? Do you think there is no chance at all for someone who cheats to understand what he did and change his behavior? Or do you view the teenager who breaks a rule or a law as a moral defective, ruined for life?

NARROWING THE WORLD
TO SIMPLE BLACK AND WHITE

Colleges want to know if you're able to take on the complexities you encounter in your world and your studies, or if you try to make everything simple. One student I know, in his personal essay, decided to relate his personal situation to *Moby-Dick,* a novel he said he'd enjoyed. Bringing in a famous novel sounded impressive, but his thinking about the novel was so narrow that it gave his readers second thoughts about his potential as a student.

He focused on the chapter that described Ahab's last attempt to hunt Moby-Dick, the dangerous white whale. Up close, Ahab gazes directly into the eyes of the giant whale and sees only "indifference." This led the applicant to explain:

> Ahab's passion gave him the advantage. The whale was complacent but not the man. And it is my own level of passionate caring that makes me a better leader than most. I am a leader with heart.

This applicant wanted to make the point that he was a passionate, caring leader, but he did it by taking one of the most challenging and admired novels in our language and reducing it to a narrow, simplistic message: *Passion is good; indifference is bad.* Now, think about that for a minute. There isn't much to this idea, is there? Do you know anyone who thinks indifference is a good quality in a leader? Is there anyone who thinks passion is always a bad quality?

In contrast, reading *Moby-Dick* offers the opportunity to think through some profound questions that occur to almost all of us at some point in our lives: Why is it that Nature or the Universe or God can appear (like the white whale) to look at humankind with "indifference"? Why does God observe suffering and injustice and then seem to do nothing? These are big questions, but this student narrowed his thinking about the novel until it became a kind of slogan for his self-proclaimed "passion." He quoted an impressive book, but he never showed his own potential to think beyond one narrow and, I have to say, pretty obvious idea.

Notice that I'm not criticizing his interpretation. It may be that this student really was as passionate about leadership as Ahab was about killing that whale. But even so, he wasn't drawing a very interesting conclusion. His idea might be right and it might be wrong, but it didn't really matter because it was so narrow. Why make an essay out of it?

Still, I don't mean to sound hard on him. He was trying to make his own original connection from personal experience to an issue of universal concern, from "me, a high school leader" to "what makes good leadership"—from a specific situation to the idea of leadership itself. That's the right goal, even if it didn't work this time. In fact, that's the gold standard of the college application. Because, if you can show broad thinking in an essay or an interview response, you have the chance to show a glimpse of your best self:

Intellectual passion

Your ability to identify with humanity as a whole

Broad thinking from what concerns you to what concerns everyone

In one brief, memorable moment, you show them you have what it takes to do college-level thinking. That can make all the difference.

So what should this student have done differently? He should have kept trying. This essay conclusion wasn't a winner, but he was moving in the right direction. If he kept working at it, this topic or perhaps another one might well have yielded an idea that would show his thinking at its best. Later in this chapter, I'll offer some specific advice on how to show broad thinking in the essay conclusion, and I'll also point out some common, misleading advice you'd do best to avoid.

Broad Thinking in the Interview

When I explain the importance of broad thinking, some students I work with imagine that I'm just talking about the written parts of the application. Admissions people can't expect every word you say in an interview to be a pearl of wisdom, can they?

Of course not. Still, the same principles of broad thinking apply to interviews. One of the main reasons colleges bother with interviews, which are time-consuming and expensive, is to get a sense of how applicants think on their feet. If they wanted prepared answers, they could send you more short-answer questions to fill out. What they're looking to see is how you roll with a thoughtful conversation, whether you let it go to unexpected places and lead you to say things you didn't know you were going to say.

One interviewer started this way:

"Tell me about yourself."

"I'm from Minnesota," Ilse answered.

"That's the 'Land of Lakes,' right?"

"Yeah. That's what it says on the license plates, anyway."

"Is that what you would have put on the license plates?"

"Well, there really are a lot of lakes."

"Do you think it made a difference to you, to grow up there?"

"I guess. If we didn't have lakes, I couldn't water-ski and ice-skate."

Ilse's answers were not incorrect, but they were narrow and factual. The interviewer was curious to know what Ilse would do when she had the chance to go beyond the facts.

"Some kids grow up in the desert," the interviewer said. "They hardly see water anywhere. But you had water all around. Did it make a difference, do you think?"

When an interviewer pushes like this, you might not have an answer right away. You might need to say, "That's an interesting question," or "No one's asked me that before." Chances are, they're not expecting you to say something brilliant. They're curious about you, and they're curious if you're comfortable with taking on a broader question, one that doesn't have a single right answer. It can help to think of this not as if you're being challenged, but as if you're getting a chance to show you can improvise.

So here's what Ilse said:

> I guess—I haven't really thought about this before—but I've met some kids who just talk about school and the mall and home, and it's like that's all there is in their world. But the way I grew up, there is this other sort of place. I mean the water, the lakes and the rivers and the things you do there, the days are different there, and it's more like things used to be. You care about the weather in a different way and what season it is. I have a pair of my grandmother's ice skates, and they fit me, and sometimes I'll look at them and think: It was the same for her, skating, even if the world is different. And she had to work hard all day just to survive. It was very special for her to have some small amount of time to just enjoy nature and her own athleticism. When I skate, I rejuvenate my mind. I wish that could have been the privilege of women then. She would have liked that. The lakes keep me connected to all of that. So I guess it does matter, having all those lakes.

PREPARE THOUGHTFUL QUESTIONS

For some applicants, I realize, the possibility of being asked to improvise a thoughtful answer to an unexpected question—with a stranger watching—is about as appealing as dental surgery. Fortunately, there is another way to show your breadth of thinking, and this can be prepared ahead of time.

Interviewers are always interested to hear what questions you'll ask them, because those questions show how you're thinking about the school and what kind of fit it might be for you. Student questions often focus directly on the student's own interests and needs. Athletes often ask, "Do you get big crowds at your ball games?" Devout students often ask, "Are professors and students understanding about religious holidays and observances?" Gay students often want to know, "Are the straight students okay about gay students?" To go further than pursuing a personal interest, you might ask questions that address your needs but also show an interest in how the community as a whole works:

"Do kids come out and support one another's activities?"

"Is there a good sense of community here? Do different sorts of people feel included?"

"How do the administration and the faculty see their roles in building a strong community?"

"What organizations or ongoing activities, in particular, bring this student body together?"

Broad Thinking in the Essay

In Chapter Two, I explained why it's so important to choose essay topics that are not just personal, but universal—in the way that type O blood is the "universal donor": Anyone can receive it. The best way to show your broad thinking in the college application is to make connections from your personal experiences to larger issues of universal concern. And this is most important at the conclusion of your essays, where your readers will be looking for you to move beyond simply describing things you've done or seen, and to say something of your own about them.

Unfortunately, applicants are often given three pieces of well-meant yet dangerous advice that can stop them from getting their most impressive thinking down on the page.

Dangerous Tip #1: "To conclude, tell 'em what you already told 'em"

If you've been taught one thing about how to structure an essay, it's likely the advice to think of an essay as having three parts. In part one, the introduction, you "tell 'em what you're going to tell 'em." Then, in part two, the body, you "tell 'em"—that is, you go into detail. Finally, in part three, the conclusion, you sum up and remind readers what they've learned—you "tell 'em what you already told 'em." This can be useful advice for longer essays, but personal statements are very short, roughly a page and a half. When readers get to page two, they still remember what they read on page one. So there is no need to sum up. In fact, if you end with a summary, you may well bore or disappoint your readers, because the conclusion is your opportunity to soar, and summaries don't soar. Instead, end with electricity; give readers at least one meaningful idea that will make the essay memorable. What kind of thought? Your own idea about the universal topic you've raised.

Dangerous Tip #2: "Show, don't tell"

Do I really mean to say "Show, don't tell" is bad advice? Hasn't just about every student writing college essays been advised Don't tell them; show them? Don't tell them you are a leader; show them. Don't tell them you are compassionate; show them. "Show, don't tell" is good advice, then—until you're writing your essay's conclusion. The conclusion is most effective when it clearly states an idea, and to do that, "telling" is not just acceptable, it's often required, if readers are going to get your point. Recall the two essays about the U.S. war in Iraq that I described earlier. One writer was worried that her country would "lose its goodness." The other said, "I want my country to be tough." But both conveyed their ideas in the "told" lines I'm quoting here, making their points clearly and memorably.

"Telling," in other words, means stating the idea directly, which often means using abstract language. The *Oxford American Dictionary* defines *abstract* as an idea that is "theoretical." You may have worked hard to "show" your experience in specific detail, but in your conclusion, in as few words as possible, your best bet is to "tell" by going into the abstract—into the theoretical (a speculative thought) about an important idea. Remember the student who concluded: "I am now an international person." He moved from specifics to an abstract thought only the rare high school kid wants to think about. But this student did and focused on one abstract idea, and in doing so he ended with one powerful thought. The kids who understand this concept are the ones against whom everyone else has to compete.

Dangerous Tip #3: "Don't try to say anything profound"

Some people who advise college-bound students hope to prevent applicants from trying too hard to say something important and making foolish generalizations. So they tell their students not to say anything at all "deep." And yet the best essays often feature bold, abstract thoughts that can also be profound. So what are you supposed to do? The truth is that most first drafts of essays either don't offer the reader any clear ideas, or if they do, these ideas are narrow, like that earlier example of the essay on *Moby-Dick*. So then you have a choice. You can back off into a safe, limited idea, or you can keep trying to say something that reflects your best thinking. That means asking yourself (or a trustworthy reader) whether you've broadened your thinking enough to reach into your experience and find an abstract, universal thought. The secrets are patience and a willingness to keep trying.

One young woman, Tammy, wrote about sometimes feeling that she was "emotionally exploited" by her boyfriends at her new school. "It's always nice to be asked out," she wrote,

> but some of these guys just seem interested in the things about a girlfriend that make them feel good. Whether it's showing her off for others to see or looking at her themselves or enjoying the things she can do for them, they don't seem to

STEPS TO SUCCESS

To take your personal feelings or concerns to a higher level, beyond yourself, try thinking of how those concerns matter to a group of people, not just to you. Then go even further and ask yourself if this concern might matter in some way universally, to all people.

see past their own private good time. With some of these guys, I feel like I'm the dessert they've ordered, and they're no more interested in talking to me than in talking to a bowl of ice cream.

In her first draft, she stuck to her personal experiences and concerns. She did a good job of "showing" with some funny examples of disastrous dates, but she had not yet moved from the personal to the universal, or from the particular to the abstract. In her second draft, she went on to link her personal experience with a more general concern about women's disadvantages in certain professions, because, as she said, "women are too often not seen, primarily, as people." I thought she had done very well, going beyond her own individual dilemma and identifying with women's experience, and then phrasing that abstract idea in one clear sentence. Nevertheless, I asked if her concern was limited just to women, or whether her topic could open all the way out to the universal, to an issue that affects all people.

She revised her conclusion, again, to invite readers to think of times when they were not "seen, primarily, as people," and whether they, too, had experienced some level of degradation by others. Exploitation, therefore, became the "heart" of her conclusion. She made the connection from the personal all the way to the universal, and the colleges were impressed. "I think exploitation against anyone," she concluded, "is a disheartening and dehumanizing experience."

CHAPTER ELEVEN

FATAL MISTAKE #11

You Waste Your Special Qualifications

Beware this error if...

—You're hoping the colleges will notice your talent—but you don't plan to do anything to get their attention

—You think of yourself as a regular college applicant, not part of any special "pool"

From early on, Maria dreamed of going to an Ivy League college. The problem was, everyone told her it was unrealistic. She had a quick mind and she was willing to work hard, but her grades were always middling and she had never tested very well. There were a lot of kids at her high school better positioned to get into top colleges.

When she came to my office the summer before tenth grade, I wanted to help her out, but as she sat there with her mother I didn't see any way to make her competitive at top schools. So I talked to her about doing the best we could, but needing to be realistic. Then I thanked her for coming in and she stood up to go.

That's when I saw something I hadn't noticed before. Maria was tall. Six feet tall and athletic. I could see the strength in her back and in her arms. She had the perfect physique for rowing. I said, "Have you ever thought about rowing crew?"

"I love crew!" she said. "I rowed in middle school. But my high school doesn't have a team. . . ."

She was from a town that I knew well, a town on a river with a town crew club. I told her, if you want to go to an Ivy, spend the next two years all year round working on crew. The Ivies care about crew. If you're competing against the regular applicant pool, I don't think I can help you, but if you're in the pool of crew recruits, you might have a chance. So what happened? It worked. She never got her SATs above the 500s, but she got selected by an Ivy League crew coach, and she proved all her doubters wrong.

You may not realize just how many students the competitive colleges admit based on the special qualifications they value, and I don't just mean athletics. A substantial percentage of an entering class gets in partly thanks to a special qualification such as: excellence in sports, the arts, or campus leadership; being the child of a graduate (a "legacy"); coming from a disadvantaged minority group; or having published writing or won science or math competitions. Does that sound like an awful lot of special exceptions? Well, from one point of view, every admission is a special exception. The majority who aren't admitted based on "special qualifications" are taken on the basis of their academic potential—that is, grades, test scores, and love of learning. That's the "pool" of applicants the colleges value most: students who will contribute academically. But there are many other gifts that students bring to the college community, and schools make an effort, sometimes very formally with a point system and sometimes more intuitively, to balance different kinds of qualifications so that every student makes some kind of special contribution to balance the class and the school.

As Maria discovered, if you change the pool of students against whom you're considered, you can change your chances of getting in. In a special pool, you no longer compete against all the other applicants to

---

DOES CHARACTER STILL MATTER?

It might seem that if you can get yourself into a good pool, then you don't have to worry about other considerations like character. In fact, the opposite is true. Because once you're in the pool of violinists or hockey players or Westinghouse finalists, you're competing against others who may look very similar to you on paper. That's when admissions people ask, "What kind of person is this violinist or hockey player or Westinghouse finalist?" Even if you're in the top academic pool, with an A average in the top AP classes and a chance of admission to the most competitive schools, you're still competing against others with exactly the same impressive qualifications. And even from the pool of the best students with the highest numbers, a college can't take them all. That's when character considerations will make you stand out from the crowd—or seal your fate.

---

the college. You essentially compete against the others in that pool. For example, some years ago one midsize Ivy League college used to take fifty promising football players a year—at least that was the scuttlebutt in admissions circles. That's a huge number. Even if there were one hundred applicants who impressed the football coaches—that is, a hundred applicants in the "football pool"—competing against each other for fifty spots, their chances of admission would be an amazing one in two, much better than normal chances outside the pool.

As important as your pool can be, there are few areas of admissions that are more misunderstood than special qualifications. Everyone may have heard about "getting in because you're an athlete," but the fact is that most kids who play sports never get considered in any special pool. Some students waste time, energy, and hope trying to demonstrate a qualification that they don't have, or that their dream schools don't care about. One student of mine banked on getting into her favorite college by means of her field hockey and lacrosse ability, but that particular college cared little about those two nonrevenue sports (sports that don't sell tickets) and gave most of their female-athletic spots to ice hockey. Another student tennis player was ranked near the bottom on her school team ladder, but insisted on believing that her preferred college would be interested in her for tennis. I warned her she had to be nationally ranked for tennis to make a difference there, but she did not listen and was later shocked at her rejection. Others imagine they will coast in on this or that special strength, only to be badly disappointed when the decisions are mailed. The point here is, you have to do your homework, or you can waste opportunities by putting your energies and time into the wrong place.

Walid was an all-conference point-guard on his high school basketball team, whom coaches thought could play for a Division I-AA college team. Walid had the backing of the basketball coach at the university he wanted to attend, and he applied for early decision at the coach's recommendation but didn't get in. He could have prevented this disappointing surprise by making sure the coach consulted with admissions ahead of time, to be sure that they were in agreement about wanting to admit him. As a student athlete trying to decide what school to commit to, it's best to know where you stand as early as possible. A school might suggest certain things you have to do as a senior to get in, like improving your ACTs or SATs or your grade point average. Or they may be discouraging, and you need to know as soon as possible if they don't expect to take you. Your guidance counselor can contact admissions for you, or if that is against their policy, you can call the person in admissions who represents the college to your school. Surprises in April are not what you want. Walid lost out because he didn't shift his commitment to another college in time.

On the other side of the coin, you may have a qualification that a particular school finds special, which the school will never notice unless you bring it to their attention. You may even have a qualification that you don't know the school would value, and the school doesn't know they need, until you use some creativity to recognize it in yourself and bring it to their attention. Some students expect colleges to discover them and their special talents, and feel that if they don't, that means they don't care. It's a mistake to expect colleges to find

---

UNMAKING THE MISTAKE

~~If you've got a special qualification, it will be obvious to the school and to you, so you can lean back and relax.~~

A special qualification is never a guarantee, but it can dramatically improve your chances—*if* you reach out to the people in a college who care about your talent, and who will bring it in the right ways to the attention of the admissions staff.

---

you. If you reach out, they will usually respond, especially if you are convincing about your interest in their college. Sometimes coaches are overwhelmed by the number of inquiries by students who are only mildly interested. Therefore, you have to be persistent and continue to e-mail them until they do respond.

WHAT MAKES A QUALIFICATION SPECIAL?

The special qualifications that colleges do or don't value may sometimes strike you as unfair or just weird. For applicants from parts of the country where crew is not a popular sport (to return to the example of Maria), a school's eagerness to admit women who can row a boat fast might seem bizarre. It's only when you see how popular the sport is at some schools, how it draws weekend visitors to the big regattas, and how it brings out school spirit in the alums who are so important to the health of the colleges that you see why it is valued. On top of that, the colleges know that when they admit a serious rower they are getting a team player with the commitment to wake up at five in the morning and go out on the water to practice even in harsh weather.

The special qualifications that colleges find most important are these:

Skill in popular varsity sports, especially "revenue sports" (sports that make money for the school from ticket sales). These are important for campus morale and for inspiring alums to make financial contributions. Athletes who come from disadvantaged families are also thought to bring valuable qualities of blue-collar toughness and commitment, plus social diversity.

Campus or community leadership.

Nationally or regionally recognized excellence of any type.

Skills in high demand at the university, which could be writing, debating, theater management, oratory ability, science competitions, organizing events or running organizations, or leadership in community service.

Membership in a disadvantaged minority.

Alumni in the family, most particularly parents.

Family history of generosity in giving time or money to the college.

Achievement in the arts, which are visible to the public and inspirational to the student body.

SPORTS

Parents of applicants sometimes tell me they worry because their kid doesn't play any sports. They don't always realize that sports make little difference in most applicants' admissions decisions. To be considered in the pool for any sport, there has to be a coach at the college looking for high-level talent that you have to offer, and that coach must put you on a special list that he or she sends to the admissions office. How does this work?

A lacrosse coach, for example, might "get" six players, which means that there are six admissions spots for which the coach's preference becomes *part* of what the admissions committee considers. That *doesn't* mean that the coach can submit a list of six names and then automatically get those six applicants in. The coach, to get six players, would probably give the admissions committee a list of two to three times that many. Athletes need to realize that although coaches have only a small number of spots they can fill, they need a long list of potential recruits to make sure they fill those spaces— since an admissions committee probably won't admit all of a coach's choices, and some who get admitted will turn the school down. It can be frustrating to applicants, but coaches have no choice except to recruit more athletes than the school can accept. On the other hand, coaches will usually be honest with you about where you stand, and it's okay for you to ask them where you lie on their list, and to take it a step further it's wise, as Walid found out, to ask them how you stand with admissions.

Out of the total list of lacrosse players for that year, then, based on all of the other usual considerations for an applicant, the admissions committee would pick six. Those players who meet admissions standards for athletes compete against each other, rather than against the entire applicant pool.

If you're a lacrosse player, your first goal would be to get on the coach's list of top choices, what is sometimes known as the "preferred list" because it's the list of recruits that the coach prefers. It may seem at this point as if the coaches have all the power, so let me tell you how it looks from their point of view. Unless you're applying to Division I schools, the coaches can't get a sure commitment from applicants in the form of a signed contract. Division I-AA or Division III coaches actually have relatively small budgets for recruiting and limited support staff. They don't have the money or the time to come out to all the high schools to scout players, and that worries them. They're hoping that you will help them find you.

Get Their Attention

So here's some very important advice: Put aside your ego. Don't wait around for them to notice how well you play. Make the first move: Send the coaches at the schools on your list a letter expressing your enthusiasm to play on their teams. Include:

1. A résumé telling them how many seasons you've played competitively, both during school and in summer, and any awards won by you or your team. Also include any objective statistics demonstrating how good you are: For track stars and swimmers include your best times; for tennis and golf, tournaments in which you've competed and your regional or national ranking. For crew give your ERG score, and for other sports, coaches like to see videos in addition to watching you play in person.

2. References who can vouch for your talents: Provide specific names, phone numbers, and e-mail addresses of the people who have coached you.

What if you don't have an impressive résumé or coaches to serve as references? You might find out what summer camps the college coach respects and make it your business to attend one no later than the summer after your junior year. These camps are places where you could be seen by a scout or coach and recruited based on your ability. Even if that doesn't happen, the coaches at the camps are known to the college coaches and could serve as convincing references. Colleges like to hear from more than your high school coach, preferably from college coaches who might have seen you at special camps or invitational competitions, or from coaches of summer league teams known to them. They can also give you a valuable assessment of the division in which you would attract the most attention.

Do you really have to do all of this? In some cases, your high school coach might have a relationship with certain college coaches, and he or she might make the connection for you. Or if you're a truly exceptional player, you might get noticed just on the basis of your reputation. But why leave it to chance, hoping you'll luck into getting "discovered," when you can give yourself the best shot by your own actions?

Interest Is Not a Commitment

Once you get their attention, you'll discover if they have some interest in you. They may tell you, "We'd love to have you here," or "I'll support you." That can be exciting to hear, but it's important to remember that interest from a coach is no guarantee that the coach will get you in or even put you on the preferred list. One athlete with whom I worked, Marc, was a legacy at a very good school whose coach said, "I'll support you." And he did want Marc on the team, but since Marc was a legacy, the coach thought he might get in anyway, so he took a gamble by keeping Marc off his preferred list. When the decisions came from the college, Marc didn't get in. He wasn't quite strong enough in the legacy pool and needed that other hook. Now he was dead in the water. He should have checked with his guidance counselor or the coach himself to find out the strength of the coach's commitment.

Another student I worked with a long time ago, a competitive horseback rider, had the support of one of the top equestrian coaches in the country. "Don't worry," the coach told me, "I'll get her in." But when decision time came, the envelope contained a wait-list letter. So I called up the coach, who said, "Oh, no! I'm so sorry. I forgot to call admissions." This is another example of how important it is to follow up right to the end when depending on special qualifications to get you in. Fortunately, the school did let that young woman in, but she suffered some anxious weeks of waiting.

These stories show how important it is to stay active in your relationship with the coaches you hope to play for. Here are some key steps:

1. **Find out how serious they are about you.** You can ask a coach, am I on your top list? Make clear that you're asking because you have a serious interest in playing for that school. Also have your school guidance counselor check with admissions to see how seriously they are committed to the coach's decision about you.

2. **Demonstrate your commitment.** Just as you're wondering how serious an enthusiastic coach really is about you, the coach wants to know how serious you are about the school. You can say: "If I'm on your preferred list, I will commit to come to your school. My college counselor will back me up on that." Then tell your college counselor what you've done. Many kids lie, I'm sorry to say, so it's important to give a coach more than just your word. Your guidance counselor's reputation is on the line, so he or she will believe your counselor.

3. **Establish a backup plan.** Once you and the coach have an understanding, tell the coach, "If you find out I'm not going to get in, let me know so I can commit to my second choice." At the same time, contact the other coaches who expressed interest in you and say, "You're one of my top choices, but I need some more time. By what date do I have to let you know that you are my first choice?"

4. **Keep your high school's college counselor up to date.** If your first-choice coach warns you that you're not going to get in, or

if your preferences change, make sure your counselor knows the score. That way you'll have extra credibility, and coaches will feel more secure in making a commitment to you. Many applicants skip this step, but it's very important.

What happens next? In Division I schools, when you and the coach reach an understanding, you sign a contract. Other schools specifically forbid contracts, but the Ivies do send out what are called "likely letters" in the fall, as early as October 1. These are letters that say you are likely to get in, very likely, as long as you don't do something terrible to spoil your record or your impression of good character. Once you receive a likely letter, you should treat it as an acceptance and you should inform coaches at your other schools, if this is your first choice. However, a likely letter does not bind you to a commitment, and coaches from other schools still have the right to pursue you. Division I-AA and Division III coaches have to depend on your honesty, and it is always a mistake not to play it straight with them. You can easily fall into a tangled mess, unless you are completely honest, and if you do demonstrate integrity, that will up your stock with any coach.

In Chapter Two I gave an example of an athlete who blew her "likely" status. She was the one who wrote in her personal essay that in high school "I studied very little. . . . I felt like a slacker." Her coach had been behind her one hundred percent, but the admissions committee felt she lacked the necessary character, and despite her likely letter she was rejected. But that's unusual. It normally takes an academic collapse or a revealed flaw in character to lose likely status.

CAMPUS AND COMMUNITY LEADERS

Whether you are editor of the school newspaper, an officer in student government, an activist in social causes, or a leader of a club or student group, you need to show that you are more than just the person who grabbed a title. Sometimes, as admissions people well know, a formal title means nothing. I remember when Phil was elected senior-prom chairman. That sounds like Phil must have had great organizational skills and a high profile among his classmates, but the truth is that Phil's family knew a high-profile rock band leader and movie star, and a lot of kids were hoping he'd perform at their prom. So they elected Phil, who asked the rock star to play for the prom. He said no. But Phil still got to call himself chairman.

Admissions people often make an effort to get the story behind your leadership titles. They'll call a high school counselor and ask: Did much happen in the school when this kid was school president? They are actually more interested to hear that you energized a group, or that you are the kind of a person who inspires an organization, than they are to hear a list of positions held.

If you are a leader of a group with a faculty advisor, you might ask your advisor to write a letter for you. Or you might approach your guidance counselor and say: Do you think I was a good leader? Is the word that I did a good job? Not all counselors realize that their opinion on a question like this matters. Also, counselors get very busy, so they may need a gentle reminder that this question is important to your application. Be sure you don't *tell them* how great a leader you were. That sort of behavior is just annoying. Ask them: "What do you think? Do you think my top schools know what kind of leader I've been?"

MINORITY STATUS

Although the public believes that being a member of any minority group puts you in a special admissions pool, that is not always the case. Generally colleges are looking for the disadvantaged or the underrepresented.

Advantage and Disadvantage

Colleges recognize that success in school, and in the college application process, comes partly as a result of the opportunities and support that are available to each applicant. Certain advantages give you a chance to do your best: if you went to a good, safe school, with access to tutors when you found a subject difficult and to test preparation courses to improve your scores; if you had parents and siblings and friends who went to college and offered their support and guidance in your high school years; if your study time was not all taken up by helping to pay the rent or to care for siblings while your parents were at work; if you had a home that was safe and quiet. However, if you come from a chaotic, unsupervised home without books or computers, and your high school was a frightening zoo where the teachers' first priority was physical safety, and the only person who could focus consistently on your success was you, then chances are your record doesn't reflect the best you could do. Under those circumstances, even getting pretty good grades is exceptional.

Colleges recognize that students who lack the advantages that encourage success in school often appear on paper to have less talent than they actually have. At Amherst, to take an example, the average SAT score is 760, but disadvantaged minorities who score in the middle six hundreds, or lower, are considered to make the cut, because they didn't have the score-raising advantages that many other applicants have. More and more, then, schools are focusing on disadvantage rather than simply minority group status. On the other hand, being both puts you in two categories of disadvantage. Here are some categories of disadvantage that make a big difference:

1. **Economic disadvantage.** If your family income is under fifty thousand dollars a year (a little more if the family is divorced), then you will be considered in the disadvantaged pool. To make this clear to the college, you only need to apply for financial aid on federal forms, which you can get from your guidance office.

From that application, the College Scholarship Service will collect information from you and then report your status to the schools. It is not necessary to write a letter explaining your situation.

2. **Native Americans.** If you have an Indian tribal number, then you are in perhaps the best pool of all, because you are rare. Proportionately, exceedingly few Native Americans apply to colleges and universities. Therefore when they do, they compete in a small pool.

If someone is a member of a minority but he or she has had all the advantages—a middle-income family life or better, good schools, a family that supported educational achievement—then being a member of a minority may mean something, but much less. In city schools or in colleges near major cities, admissions can be just as tough for well-off minorities as anyone else.

Underrepresented Minorities

In addition to the disadvantaged pool, which makes spaces for students whose records don't tell the whole story about them, some schools seek to admit members of minorities who are not well-represented in the school's student body. They want all of their students to benefit from the broader range of perspectives and the more complete sense of the American experience that comes from studying and living with a more diverse group. In small, northern, relatively rural schools, for example—at Middlebury, Colby, Bates, Bowdoin, Lawrence, Hamilton, or Carleton, even African-American and Hispanic applicants from relatively privileged backgrounds might be considered to have a special qualification, because they get relatively few applications from people of color. Jews and Asians, who are not usually treated as minorities anymore, may be especially welcome at schools where they are not

---

STEPS TO SUCCESS

I f you have questions about your minority status, there is a minority representative at each admissions office and he or she is the person to ask.

---

well represented. City schools may give special consideration to students from rural backgrounds, and so forth.

Danger: Questionable claims of minority status

John wanted to get into a school, in a posh suburb outside Boston, that he thought was beyond his reach. So he falsely checked off "African-American" on his application. He got in, but his high school counselor was surprised and did some investigating to find out why, and John was exposed. John had been resentful of affirmative action and, when on the line, tried to justify his actions, but his devious behavior cost him a year before another college would consider him.

UNUSUAL TALENTS

I worked with a student who loved the technical aspects of theater—lighting design, sound design, all of the backstage craft that helps the actors look good. The student wanted to go to a prominent small New England college, but his chances seemed poor. Still, he had a gift for tech work, so we asked the theater arts teacher at his high school to talk to the theater departments of various colleges, and sure enough, that made the difference. They had lots of people who wanted to be onstage, but a shortage of technical support.

How did I know his tech background could count as much as other special qualifications? I didn't, so the student and I explored it, reaching out to theater directors at all the colleges on his list. If you have any unusual skills or qualities that your college counselor or high school faculty members can vouch for, it's worth finding out (during campus visits or by phone) whether your top schools might value them enough to have a pool for your special attribute. Orchestras are sometimes looking for a specific instrument; club sports sometimes shift to varsity status, creating a special need for players. So if you are an outstanding French-horn player, let's say, you should directly contact administrators of the orchestra and send in a tape of your playing to music departments (and be sure admissions knows you have done this). A coach may need a manager; a religious community may be lacking in leadership and in numbers; there may not be enough political activists on campus. Two of my Orthodox Jewish students got into their top choices by making their applications known to heads of college Hillel Houses. Two opera singers got into their first choices at Yale and Rice by virtue of tapes and recommendations sent to music departments.

Sometimes the administration feels a shift in the tone of the campus that they don't like. Recently, one prominent school saw their student body as too materialistic and they went looking for more service-minded students. Another was concerned about the amount of misbehavior among freshman boys and began to look more carefully for greater maturity in their male applicants. Actually, all colleges look for social maturity as well as intellectual maturity. Transfers and gap-year candidates, therefore, can have an advantage, since they tend to be older and more mature. When maturity becomes apparent in students' applications, the personal attributes associated with being a little "older" can also be a "hook."

Danger Sign: Outdated reputations

The reputation of a school your parents knew in their era may no longer represent the nature of the college, or the kind of student they seek. Don't rule out schools on the basis of a previous generation's ideas of who does and doesn't go there. Some schools that might fall into this category are Rollins, Tulane, SMU, Dartmouth, Holy Cross, Mills, Brandeis, the Cal system, the Virginia state system, Vassar,

Washington and Lee, Middlebury, St. Lawrence, Hamilton, Connecticut College, Bates, and Colby. These days they may surprise you. Sometimes colleges have reputations of being party schools, places anyone can get into. Some might have, at one time, lacked social diversity, gender balance, or gender compatibility. Others may be more intellectual than their competitive level indicates. You have to evaluate a college—particularly its student body—for yourself, by visiting the campus when the students are there.

LEGACIES

If one or both of your parents went to a college where you're applying, your chances of admissions are significantly greater. Sometimes in top schools, as many as fifty percent are taken from that pool, rather than around ten or twenty to thirty percent depending on the school. In theory, a sibling at a college makes you a "half legacy," but that's not as powerful a hook as a parent, and many schools feel they only have to take one applicant from each legacy family. Still, you should mention all family members who went to the school, even grandparents and aunts and uncles, just in case it helps. There is space for legacy information in the application form.

Colleges have to favor parental legacies because legacy families are their main source of endowment, much of which goes for scholarships. This enables a college to be competitive among its best applicants, which ironically brings socioeconomic diversity to the college.

DEVELOPMENT CASES

Development cases are applicants whose families can potentially benefit the college community through their generosity in funding libraries, sports centers, and other capital projects. Their ability to add to scholarship funds in particular justifies their special status to college administrators. If you are a legacy and your family has a history of philanthropic giving to a school where you apply, or even to other institutions such as hospitals or museums or schools, you may be placed in the development pool.

It may or may not help you. Thirty years ago, at some schools, your academic record didn't have to be very good if you were a development case, but now you have to be competitive academically to be considered, and to demonstrate that you contributed in personal ways to your high school. (Being in the development pool may actually hurt you with some admissions people, because they may feel you already have enough advantages and don't need a high-status school as well.) If you do get in from the development pool, it generally means you had qualities that the admissions committee liked, as you had to overcome their reluctance to give you an edge.

Often colleges do not like to take marginal legacies under the

WHAT IF YOU HAVE A FRIEND WITH "PULL"?

Every year, I hear parents say, "Don't worry, I know a trustee of the school. He's got pull with admissions and he says if my kid is committed to the school, he's in, no sweat." I have to tell them that only in rare cases does it work like that—very rare. If the student is on the edge of qualifying for admission on his or her own, it can happen that "pull" makes the difference, but not if the college would have to lower its standards. Admissions people may well make special room if the applicant is the child of a trustee or alumnus who has worked hard for the college, but for mere friends of trustees or large donors, the college's attitude is usually "It's not his kid; he'll get over it." If you're applying to a school that's competitive enough to have to turn down qualified kids—and that's a lot of schools these days—you can forget about pull. I've seen famous politicians, movie stars, and even royalty use their names and their pull and get nowhere.

umbrella of early decision or early action, as that is a "noisy" acceptance. In the fall, the whole high school community is focused on who gets in early decision. Even for regular decision in the spring, everyone knows where everyone else got in or didn't. College decisions are dramatic, so to avoid public scrutiny, a college might wait until June or July, when the school has disbanded for the summer, to offer admissions to a marginal legacy. This is known as a "quiet" admission.

You might not feel comfortable with this kind of advantage, but more is expected of students from affluent families. You are held to a higher standard, and alumni support makes it possible for greater numbers of scholarship students to attend. It would be a greater evil, I think, if colleges couldn't raise enough money from their alumni to offer scholarships to the disadvantaged. And you still have to stand out, on your own, in what is usually a competitive pool.

Once, a highly competitive university asked me to keep a development family calm by reassuring them that their child would receive a delayed acceptance in July. This college wanted to be exceedingly "quiet" about this case, because the family was highly powerful in the college's own political arena. In June, the father came to see me. Standing with his face about two inches from mine, he said, "Dunbar, you better be right!" Looking him straight in the eye, I responded confidently that I was. But the college did not take that student in July or even in August. They waited until September, a few days before classes began. And although I was safely hidden away on a graduate school campus, I was looking over my shoulder all summer.

THE ARTS

Arts performances and exhibitions are some of the most memorable ways people get introduced to a school, and when they are good, that helps shape the school's public reputation as well as the morale of its own students. When applying to college, applicants in both sports and the arts need to take a similar approach. Just as athletes demonstrate their talents by documenting their times, scores, and overall records, artists need to put together a portfolio that shows what they can do. If you're a musician, send a professionally taped recording of your instrument or voice, and inquire about auditions. If you're a painter, send slides or digital reproductions of your paintings. If you're a theater tech person, document your contributions. And so on. Just as with athletes, if you can make it into the pool for a particular type of art, you can change your chances dramatically.

Once during my years as a college counselor at Phillips Academy, Andover, I was in the admissions office at a first-tier university on the very day they turned down one of our students. She had SAT scores in the low 600s and an okay GPA. When we asked about her they said, "Sorry. She just doesn't cut the mustard." Competing in the academic pool, she couldn't make it. Then we realized that the admissions committee didn't know about the tape. The student had not followed through to make sure. When this became clear, one of us said, "Wait, she's a talented opera singer. She's worked with one of the best opera companies in the country. She sent the music department a tape. What happened to that tape?"

The admissions committee had no record of the tape. Immediately, at our urging, they called up the music department, where the tape was still sealed in its envelope. No one had heard it. The music professor on the phone said they would listen to it and call admissions back. Twenty minutes later the call came. They said, "Take her."

This story demonstrates several important considerations for applicants who excel in the arts. If you're hoping to compete in an arts pool, you need to:

1. Collect a portfolio of examples of your artistic work, including samples of as broad a range of styles or genres as possible. If you're a singer or a musician, send a professional-quality

recording (or the best-quality recording you can afford). If you're a visual artist, send digital images or slides. If you're a dancer or an actor, send a video. If you're a writer, send published pieces or manuscripts with teacher comments. Those who can perform well in more than one form (two instruments, jazz and classical, poetry and prose) should send examples of both. Colleges are often particularly interested in students whose work goes beyond being beautiful or technically impressive, and who are starting to use their talents to make a larger point or to communicate their feelings—they admire art that says something significant, socially or personally. Be always ready to explain what you are expressing, either emotionally or intellectually. That could make the difference. Dance, for instance, is a major at some colleges, because it is an art form that can communicate ideas.

2. If you visit the school campus, stop in at the specific department where you hope to study and ask to whom you should send your portfolio. If you aren't going to visit, then call the department and ask. When you send in your work, include a cover letter explaining that you are an applicant. Why shouldn't you send your work to the admissions department? Admissions people are not experts in the arts, and usually they will defer to the judgment of professors.

3. Include a separate letter with your application to let the admissions committee know you have submitted a portfolio of your work and that they should expect to hear a response from the department where you sent it. Include the date you mailed the materials.

4. Let your guidance counselor know you have submitted a portfolio, and give him or her a copy of your letter to the admissions office.

5. In your application, include a résumé that notes your performances or publications or displays of your work. List any prizes
or other forms of recognition as well as any special training
you have received. Make clear that your involvement with the
arts is a year-round commitment.

6. Request recommendation letters from relevant teachers, directors, and others who can speak to the quality of your work and
your promise. These should go to the admissions office, like
other recommendation letters, with copies to the specific
department(s) where you've sent a portfolio.

7. Don't assume that because you have sent in your work, anyone
has seen or heard it. It is acceptable to follow up with the admissions department to make sure that your materials have
gotten some attention at least a month before decisions are
coming in the mail.

Feeling Awkward?

You may find preparing a portfolio and sending it to experts you
haven't met makes you uncomfortable. That's no surprise, really.
Many students with real talent in the arts feel uncomfortable, and by
choice or avoidance they don't send a portfolio. That's a shame, because it makes them seem either much less talented or much less
committed than they actually are. The students who overcome their
self-consciousness then get an extra advantage, because there are
fewer applicants in their pools. For all these reasons I say: Do it. It
can only help. Remember that the people who see your work are not
going to be deciding your future as an artist. They're only considering whether they can see already how you would benefit their department and community. Not everyone's promise comes across in a
portfolio, and many fine artists were not recognized as teenagers.

STEPS TO SUCCESS

Your special qualifications can only help you if you bring them to the attention of admissions people. Early on in the application process:

- Review the list of special qualifications and consider which, if any, apply to you.
- Don't rely on colleges to notice your qualifications. Bring your gifts to the attention of those at your favorite colleges who would appreciate them.

Don't build this up as the ultimate test of your gifts. This is just a chance to give your college application a boost. And simply sending in your work can help you because your work helps show what you care about, which can enrich an admissions committee's sense of you overall.

CHAPTER TWELVE

FATAL MISTAKE #12

You Don't Learn from Rough Times

Beware this error if . . .

—*Your record reflects a rough period in your life, whether from illness or family upset*
—*You've been "in trouble" at school*

Illness or death in the family. Divorce. Problems with drugs and alcohol. Cheating. Suspensions, expulsions, legal consequences. In the chapter on "Going Negative" I warned you against *seeming* too negative, whether out of habit, peer pressure, or just a passing mood. But what if, like a lot of people, you have some real negatives in your background? Both bad luck and bad judgment can affect school performance, sending a student into an academic tailspin. What if you've gotten into trouble—or trouble has come knocking on your door? Do admissions people sympathize?

The answer is, not much.

When your difficulties are due to bad fortune (death, divorce, or illness), you're likely to get a little sympathy. Still, the main response I hear from admissions people is "That's too bad, but we'll take the kid who's resilient, who went through an illness or emotional trauma and still got A's."

SHOW YOUR RESILIENT SIDE

What if you don't have the high marks? You can show your resilience in other ways. In every experience of rough times there are always at least two stories to tell; you need to understand which story the colleges want to hear. It's not the story of the terrible things that befell you, it's the story of what you, personally, did in response. Not the story of the kid who's been knocked down, but the story of the kid who got back up again.

Jasper was a student of mine who suffered from dyslexia, though he wasn't properly diagnosed until his junior year. When he got appropriate help, his whole feeling for school changed, and a struggling, resentful student blossomed in math and physics. His teachers grew excited about his potential. Their letters on his behalf emphasized their new sense of his capabilities. In his personal essay, however, instead of writing about his intellectual awakening, he wrote about the trials of his early years: how he'd struggled with academics and felt that nothing could inspire him. He detailed his failures, his embarrassments, and his low self-esteem in the angry years when school made him feel stupid and helpless. He relived the worst of his experience.

Writing the essay made him feel better, and his family found it moving. His mother even wept when she read it. Yet to the admissions committees, the message seemed to be that the condition was still the center of his life. He barely mentioned the shift in his experience and his newly discovered intellectual interests. He seemed stuck in his troubles. I suggested that he do the following to change his emphasis:

- Cut back on the long, involved descriptions of hard times and failings.
- Develop the story of how you found solutions.

It's like that old expression I mentioned earlier, about when life gives you lemons. Admissions people do want to hear honestly about the lemons in your life, but what they really want is your recipe for lemonade.

At first, my approach made Jasper nervous. If he changed the emphasis, he said, wouldn't that mean the colleges would miss part of the whole story? Was that really what I meant? I told him, yes, it was. Because, as I've said before, the colleges have only a short chance to get to know you, so you need to seize your chance to share the most important parts of your story. It can be helpful to think about what a personal essay or interview is *not:*

You may talk about personal concerns, but it's not a therapy session. It may be useful to remind yourself of the reason you're there: not for them to assist you with personal concerns, but for you to help them imagine the sort of college student you will be.

You should be honest, but it is not a confessional, not the place to bare the worst of yourself or to ask forgiveness.

You can be friendly, but it is not like a conversation with a friend where you can "say anything."

NOT EVERYONE HAS A DRAMATIC COMEBACK

Am I saying that you are required to have a story of an amazing comeback against terrible odds? No, of course not. More important than the results, however, is your approach, how you cope with what you've gone through. One applicant I worked with had suffered a low period—a whole semester, actually—that could have made for a long, harrowing story. When she applied to colleges, she was still anticipating low grades and a generally disappointing semester. She was no phoenix rising from the ashes, at least not yet. But she wrote about her rough time with her emphasis on her response to it:

> My parents separated last summer and this fall I caught mononucleosis and missed a month of school. My grades reflect it in every class. Still, I loved a lot of those classes, and I kept up with them to a level just a little under a hundred percent. My grades won't be great, but I'm still enjoying my classes and contributing in the ways I can.

Notice how she kept the focus off the setbacks and on her response, even though her response was still happening. She kept her description of the dip in her grades general and brief. She didn't apologize, ask her reader to forgive her, or offer promises about the future. She did state clearly what had happened and then moved on to reaffirm her feelings for her classes and her commitment to them. Her mature and forward-looking approach seemed to impress her readers. Despite the bad semester, she got into her first-choice college.

HAS YOUR JUDGMENT IMPROVED?

Besides wanting to know if you are resilient, admissions people want to know about the choices you make under pressure—that is, your judgment. Especially if you've made bad choices in the past, such as cheating, stealing, or abusing alcohol or drugs, they want to know if you've learned enough from the experience to make different judgments the next time. This is often their biggest concern when students get into trouble. Why? In their view, generally, a young person is not yet fully formed. A student may make a really bad decision, but if that individual is genuinely remorseful and can learn to see the significance of what he or she did wrong, then he or she may well grow to become as responsible as others, perhaps even more so. Colleges tend to give a second chance when applicants show new growth and responsibility.

One student, Lisa, was caught sharing her answer sheet with a friend during the PSATs. She knew this episode from tenth grade was part of her school record, so she tried to address it in an essay: "I would not have cheated if I had fully known the consequences," she wrote, "and I intend never to cheat again."

That statement killed her. She appeared to be saying only that she regretted getting caught. Now, perhaps when she said, "if I'd known the consequences," she meant to include the harm that cheating does to everyone—her fellow students, her school, even her community—but she didn't say so, and that left admissions people lots of room to doubt her. She did not seem to understand, even a few years later, how unfair to her fellow students it was to cheat, or how damaging cheating was to her school, both to its reputation among outsiders and to the spirit of shared intellectual exploration within her classes. (One cheater in a school can put pressure on everyone else, making them feel, "If others are doing it, shouldn't I do it too? Otherwise I'll be at a disadvantage.")

Lisa seemed unaware of any issue beside her own wish not to get caught again. In this case, several schools she applied to decided that she did not have the judgment to join their community, and they turned her down.

Lisa's lack of mature judgment was pretty easy to spot. The more dangerous group of students who break rules or laws, from the colleges' view, are the ones who don't get caught, at least not yet. For this reason, as I suggested in Chapter Five, "You Seem Like a Threat," colleges scrutinize your application for signs of hostility, dishonesty, or selfishness that could signal more serious threats to come. What is cheating, after all, but extreme selfishness? Logically, unselfish people with a strong feeling for their communities are less likely to indulge in devious behavior. And even if you have gotten into trouble, you can still work to demonstrate the generous, honest, involved side of yourself.

In an effort to weed out those applicants who still lack good judgment, admissions people look for warning signs in your application:

- Blustery and overstated claims mark you as too childish to make sense of your experience: "I learned my lesson and I will never forget it. I'll never again do anything dishonest or destructive." A statement like this is just too simplistic to take seriously.

• Self-righteous anger or clichéd life lessons imply you haven't learned mature judgment: "What I did might have been wrong, but isn't it even worse to put a permanent blot on the record of a young person just trying to build his future?" Here the essay writer sounds as if he thinks the real crime was that the school enforced its rules.

WILL YOU WORK TO SOLVE SERIOUS PROBLEMS?

Some kinds of trouble suggest to colleges that an applicant has a more serious problem than an immature lack of judgment. One student I worked with beat up a boy who had apparently been disrespectful to his girlfriend, putting his victim in the hospital. Another, a girl from a wealthy family, got into a pattern of shoplifting from department stores. Another was caught by the police after breaking the windows of a row of parked cars. In cases like these, colleges will worry that the applicants are not people they can trust, at least not at this time in their lives. These serious troubles include:

acts of violence

vandalism

selling drugs

chemical dependency

serious theft

long periods of poor academic performance (more than just a bad grade or disappointing term)

Yet even in these situations, the colleges usually respect and welcome the individual who will work to overcome his or her flaws. I've found that even in very serious cases, if a student is willing to make full use of the help and resources that are available, especially therapy, the colleges will usually allow a reapplication after a year or sometimes two, depending on the nature of the "crime." What you do with that time in between should be approved by colleges to which you intend to apply, but generally colleges are very forgiving if the student shows remorse and personal growth.

One boy, for instance, plagiarized an essay as a senior and had his admission to a top school deferred for one year. Having been a top student, he wasn't required to do any academic work during that year, but he was expected to perform considerable social service. In another case, a legacy candidate who had a C+ average in high school was required by Harvard to get A's for two years at another institution. He did, and got in.

In yet another case, I worked with a student named Todd who wanted to go to his father's alma mater, which was considered the best public college in their state. However, Todd had a serious problem with high school attendance. Eventually he was caught outside of class, getting stoned on school property. When I met him, he was worried that between his low grades and his illicit behavior he had blown his chance to go to his first-choice school.

I told him that he might still be able to get his wish, if he would attend the summer program at his first-choice school, then start the fall semester at another of the state schools. If he stayed away from drugs and out of trouble and brought up his grades, I thought he'd have a good chance to transfer to his first choice for sophomore year. I also suggested to him, as his school guidance counselor and his parents had done, that he meet with a therapist. He agreed.

When I contacted his therapist later in the year, however, I learned that his attendance there was even less reliable than at school. Todd told me he felt uncomfortable with the idea of seeing a therapist and rationalized that, because he'd had trouble for such a long time, he couldn't see how meeting and talking to someone was going to change things. Therefore, he did not fully open up to his therapist. I suggested that the college was hoping to see evidence of newfound balance and maturity, and that it is a sign of maturity to acknowledge parts of ourselves that we want to change and to work to do so. I said I didn't know if this therapist could help him, but at least by attending his therapy sessions, he was keeping a promise to his high school and his potential college. He would show his commitment by showing up for his meetings and fully engaging his psychologist, and in that way he would build the trust of his high school guidance counselor and college admissions committees and convince them that he could and would look at himself objectively. This would at least gain him the trust of a college. I told him that in thirty-plus years as an admissions counselor, commitment to therapy was the only way I'd ever seen anyone in his situation turn it around.

STEPS TO SUCCESS

If a college is aware of serious trouble that casts doubt on your character, the best you can do is to show them your willingness to work on the problems and change.

- With help from your family, seek out guidance both in school and from an outside therapist.
- Ask your college counselor and your therapist to apprise the colleges of the steps you have taken. Your guidance counselor can reassure the admissions people and help you decide whether it is appropriate to put your therapist in contact with the college's counseling staff.

Eventually he did trust himself and his therapist enough to discover the fears that kept his confidence low and his attendance spotty. He was able to learn to respond to those fears in new ways, rather than with his old habit of sneaking off to get high. In time he discovered that he had some real intellectual ability and that he could excel academically in some areas. Once his desired college understood what he had gone through and saw his academic surge, they admitted him the next year.

If you've got some negatives in your school record and you feel doubtful that colleges will grant you a second chance, it might make you feel better to think of it this way: They've already given you a second chance. They know that it's especially hard to apply when you feel there's something wrong that you have to make up for. The way you handle yourself in the application process is itself a chance to show how you've grown in understanding and maturity, and to suggest how much more you could grow and learn—at the right school.

CHAPTER THIRTEEN

FATAL MISTAKE #13

Sitting There, Waiting

Beware this error if . . .

—*Your early application is deferred until regular admissions in the spring*

—*You receive a wait-list letter from your first-choice school*

There's no getting around it: If you get deferred or put on a wait list, you'll feel bad. It's disappointing not to be accepted right away, and you may well feel hurt or angry. Some applicants, discouraged by ominous statistics, turn passive and simply wait, hoping for the best. Some reject the school in return, saying, "If they don't want me the way I am, then I don't want them."

I understand these responses, but to me they miss the point. As we've seen, an admissions committee's chance to get to know you is brief and artificial. They *can't* reject you the way you really are because *they never got to know you the way you really are.* They only know the little you've shown them in this strange ritual called college admissions. So although it may feel like a rejection, that wait-list letter or deferral is something very different. It means that the college

UNMAKING THE MISTAKE

~~Being put on a wait list or deferred is a rejection.~~

A wait list or deferral letter is a request for more information. It's up to you to show them more of your best self.

still doesn't know enough about you to make an informed decision, yes or no. They're hoping that rather than falling silent or pushing them away, you'll come closer, so they can know you better. They may not be able to go to their wait list, and although this involves some emotional risk to you—the doors may close no matter what you do—let them know more about you. Even if they say no this time, they will know you better the next year, if you apply again.

There *is* good news. They haven't said no. There must be reasons they find your application appealing, because they could've sent a rejection letter—but they didn't. They've said "maybe" or "not yet" or "show us a little more of what you can do." And so the trick is to stop waiting around and take action. How? Try thinking of your disappointing letter as a kind of acceptance: You've been accepted for a correspondence course, and if you earn a top grade in that course, you can still get in. In this new course, you must undergo a challenging setback—the college of your choice has not accepted you yet—and show you can meet that challenge by continuing to perform well at school and demonstrating your extraordinary character. The worst thing you can do is just sit there, waiting. The school has asked for more information, so don't deprive them of the one thing that might help them say yes.

To be honest, depriving them of what they want or telling them off might feel pretty good right now. If you're feeling hurt, disappointed, or embarrassed to be kept waiting, you may want to vent some anger. That's fine—just don't do it in such a way that the school can find out about it and feel attacked.

Don't give the college the silent treatment.

Don't put down the college to your guidance counselor or anyone else who might talk to an admissions person and pass along your angry words.

And of course, don't send them an angry letter suggesting that they made a mistake.

The risk with anger, as natural and as normal as it may be, is that the school you're still hoping to impress might mistake these reactions for evidence of exactly those character flaws that can be fatal to an application. Here are some potentially suicidal approaches, and why the colleges might view them as evidence of unacceptable character flaws:

Don't go silent. *They know that it's disappointing not to be let in right away—they disappoint hundreds or thousands of kids every year. So they'll be looking for evidence of what you might learn from a disappointment. If you show them nothing in response, they can only guess that you've learned nothing and that you haven't cultivated your ability to learn from life's setbacks.*

Don't argue. *No one ever argued her way into an acceptance to college, or defended herself so brilliantly that an admissions person said, "Wow, you're right. We goofed. You're in!" This may seem obvious, but it can be surprisingly easy to fall into what sounds like arguing without even realizing it. Emotions can run high when you and your friends are hearing from colleges, and even innocent remarks and questions may easily sound like a challenge to someone in admissions. So if you're in communication with the school in any way, even for a minute on the phone:*

- Don't say, "I'm surprised I didn't get in."

- Don't tell stories about other applicants you've heard were admitted with a lower class rank than yours, or from a less competitive school than yours, or who own hamsters or other small rodents whose fur isn't as shiny as the fur on your pets, or any other comparison. To them it just sounds like hostility toward your fellow students.

- Don't call to check where you are on the list. A college is not a restaurant and admissions people are not hostesses who have promised you a table. (If you are at all condescending to anyone in the admissions office, it suggests not just disrespect but an inability to imagine what they're going through. They are doing their job, after all, which is to evaluate your application as well as they can. If you treat them disrespectfully, they may take that as a sign of social insensitivity and expect that you will treat others at the college poorly too.)

- Don't apologize or offer explanations for anything in your record. It's no help to say, "I know I got a B-minus in math but it was a senior slump and that teacher is a tough grader and anyway I'm going to major in French." If you want to raise concerns about your record, discuss them with your guidance counselor. The counselor might choose to raise them in a direct conversation with the admissions people.

In all of these cases, if you sound like you're arguing (whether or not you mean to) you will probably annoy whoever is on the receiving end of your complaints, and you will force that person to show extra patience to make up for your lack of mature restraint. That's what parents have to do with small children. In this way, your angry response suggests Fatal Mistake #7, emotional dependency—you are acting like a small child who depends on others to manage your

UNMAKING THE MISTAKE: ANGER

What *can* you do with your anger and your disappointment about not getting in right away?

- Find family or friends who sympathize and tell them what you *wish* you could tell the admissions committee.
- If you're really down, try talking to a counselor (I mean a therapist, not your college counselor) to get to the root of it.
- Take that frustrated feeling of wishing you could *do something* and direct that energy back into working on your application, where it can still do you some good.

unrestrained emotions. This gives admissions people a new reason to turn down your application.

SIX WAYS TO HELP YOUR CASE

1. Let your college counselor know that your first choice *is* still your first choice, so he or she can pass the word along. Reach out to your counselor; stop by for a chat and send a follow-up note afterward so he or she can add it to your file.

2. Write to the college directly and let them know you still hope to go there, and that your counselor will verify your commitment. If you were deferred from early application to regular application, send a letter in February. If you receive a wait-list letter, return the included postcard right away, and follow up with a letter. What is appropriate in this sort of follow-up letter? It should say that the school is still your first choice, and that the year has been going well for you. Include any news that is relevant to your application. For example:

- new activities
- new honors or awards
- classes you're especially excited about

3. Ask another teacher to write a letter to admissions on your behalf. (If you're an athlete, stay in touch with the coach.) Teacher letters are always significant to admissions officers—and they can help. Don't worry about sending too many. Admissions people don't want to hear from trustees or VIPs, but they do value letters from anyone who has taught you in the classroom. You might ask a teacher who has gotten to know you better since you sent in your application, or one who can describe some qualities that might not already be clear.

   Remember, when you approach your teachers, they do not owe you a letter. It's a favor. Sometimes it's helpful to feel a teacher out by telling your story. "I heard from X College. I'm on the wait list." If the person takes an interest, you might explain that you wish you had the chance to let the school know more about you, especially when it comes to something that the teacher knows. At that point you might ask whether the person would be willing to write a letter, if she thinks she could add something significant to your application.

4. Review your application with a college counselor if possible, and look for inconsistencies. Often what sinks a good application is a gap between the way you present yourself and the way other elements of your application present you: You don't seem to be the person you've claimed. For example, Ray had a high class rank at a good school and he described himself as "passionate about the environment." Yet when admissions people got to know his file, they learned that he didn't participate in many environmentally oriented extracurriculars, and that neither his college counselor nor his college admissions readers felt they saw much depth of knowledge or special involvement in that area. Ray was rejected from all but his safety school, so in

his first year of college, I encouraged him to act on his feelings and join environmental organizations and also to read more widely in the field. He'd always had an interest, but now he was really doing something about it. This change showed up in his transfer application, and the next year he was able to transfer to his original first-choice school.

5. Go to the school. Don't call and ask for an appointment. They will tell you not to come. Stop in at the admissions office, unannounced. Don't say that you'd like an interview or that you want to find out if you're likely to get in. Schools don't generally offer extra interviews or talk to students face-to-face about their chances. Instead, tell the receptionist, "I'm on the wait list and I just want to talk to someone in admissions because I have questions to ask them. I have some major decisions to make."

Once there, let the admissions person you speak to see how interested you are in the school and how mature you are in your attitude. Zoë, for example, took the bull by the horns when she was wait-listed by one of the most competitive schools in the country. After the list was closed in June, terminating her application, she pushed her hurt and her nervousness aside and called the admissions office. She explained that she wanted to meet with the director of admissions.

To her surprise, he agreed. In that meeting she gave the director her reasons for preferring his college, and asked what she would have to do to get in. What could she do in another year or two to improve her chances? She felt that this school and this student body were such a good fit for her that they were worth waiting for. Was it totally unrealistic for her to continue to try? she asked. Was there a specific weakness she might identify and overcome?

The director was dazzled by her maturity and commitment, and most of all, I think, by her patience. She knew where she wanted to go for the right reasons. She wanted to be among bright, socially mature students, and she had the patience to do what was required and to wait as long as necessary to realize her goals. These are qualities that augur success in almost every aspect of life. At the end of their conversation, he offered her a guaranteed acceptance for the following year.

In most cases you won't get a guarantee, but often you will be told what you can do to become a stronger candidate the next time. You may at the same time establish a contact in the admissions office who knows you and who may very well become an advocate for your application.

6. If you can't have a personal meeting, take the same approach in a letter. There is no magic formula that convinces a school how well suited it is for you, and you for it, but there are some approaches I'd encourage you to avoid. Very often, I've seen students take this unhelpful approach, which Liz tried in her letter:

> Your decision to defer me has inspired me to new academic efforts and productivity. I have been considerably more focused, and my teachers are impressed. I believe that your decision was the best thing that could happen, because it put me into overdrive!

This letter had been screened by her English teacher, who found it "cogent and well-written." It was reviewed by a distinguished alumnus of the college, who said it was "impressive." Liz was proud of it, because it showed her motivation. Yet the admissions committee was not impressed. To them, saying "this setback made me work harder" suggested that the applicant did not have an inner passion for academic work, and required outside prodding for motivation. It suggested two fatal mistakes at once, a lack of both true intellectual passion (see Chapter Three) and of emotional independence (see Chapter Seven). Her drive did not come from within. Had she been genuinely interested in her subjects, they reasoned, she wouldn't have needed a deferral to get her motivated.

For the same reason, it is dangerous to draw attention to improved grades. "Since you put me on the wait list, my grades have improved" implies that you see grades as a means to an end, and raises questions about how ethical you would be in pursuit of better grades. One admissions person told me, "When I read a letter like that, I can just see the student sucking up to teachers and pressuring them to help get her in."

If candidates, however, when rejected at a given college, show perseverance in a mature way, they can often get there. Most of their peers don't have the patience to postpone gratification. They want to begin college when their friends do, or they just can't live with any more uncertainty. They don't have the patience or the imagination to keep working at it. Therefore, students like Zoë stand out among their age group. They appear more mature, and in June and July when admissions officers are under less pressure, they get a more careful look. The willingness to be different and mature usually pays off.

OTHER OPTIONS: TRANSFERS

Even if you don't get off the wait list, transferring is an option if you can imagine starting college somewhere else and then making a change. No matter what may be missing from your application, you can develop it at another college. Once you're at the other college, you may find that it suits you well—we all get hung up on names and prestige, but there are many, many fine schools in this country. If you still feel that your first-choice school is compelling for you, you can apply again. It comes down to patience, dedication, and character—all manifestations of maturity.

STEPS TO SUCCESS

When colleges ask applicants to wait for the acceptance they want so much, most don't have the maturity to postpone gratification. Most applicants want to begin college when their friends do or they feel they can't live with any more uncertainty. Maybe they don't have the patience or the imagination to keep working at it. But if you persevere, you may find that in June and July when admissions officers are under less pressure, your application will get a more careful look. The willingness to be patient and pursue your own goals often pays off.

OTHER OPTIONS: TAKING TIME OFF

Another alternative is to take a year off from school. You might get a full-time job, learn a foreign language, find an internship in a field that interests you, or volunteer for a cause in which you believe. Columbia even has a special program called General Studies, for which one becomes eligible after one full year away from academia. Why does Columbia value students who are willing to take a year away from academia? It's often a maturing experience to have to live outside the structure of college life and to be away from your own age group. The kids who are most adamant about following the expected and popular route, and going straight from high school into college, are often more immature and insecure than they realize, and therefore unrealistic about their own readiness for college.

Colleges want their students to be as mature and as broadly experienced as possible. In fact, I remember the first time I worked with a student—a relatively immature legacy—who got into a top school and then decided to take a year off. I was embarrassed because I had assured the college that the student in question was definitely coming to them in the fall if she got in. So I called the head of admissions to apologize. His words were comforting: "Don't worry, Don. Ask her if she would like to take two years."

CONCLUSION

In the Introduction, I challenged you to find at least seven mistakes in a single sentence taken from an actual personal statement. Before you had read this book, that would probably have been impossible, but if you've learned to recognize the Thirteen Fatal Mistakes, you should be ready now for the challenge. You know that a single phrase, sometimes even a single word, can put concern and doubt in an admissions person's mind. Some of these mistakes will seem obvious to you now. And some may seem very small, almost too small to bother with, but as even this one sentence shows, the danger is that even the smallest, subtlest mistakes may lead an admissions person to ask further questions, and in time add up to a decisive change in your reader's view of you.

Here is the sentence again: *At my highly regarded private school, I am being prepared to excel at a superior college, which will hopefully bring me success and happiness in the future.* Let's look at it a few words at a time, to see the worries it might plant in the minds of college admissions officers.

1. **Dependency.** *"At my **highly regarded private school** . . ."* This applicant introduces himself, first and foremost, in terms of his prestigious school. Who is he? Well, he tells us, he's Mr. Highly Regarded Private School. This makes him sound dependent (Fatal Mistake #7) on the school and its reputation for his own self-image. This suggestion of dependence is worsened by

his passive way of describing his education: "I am **being pre-pared** to excel," he writes, which "will **bring me** success." He sounds as if he thinks education is something that will be delivered when he calls for it, like a pizza he's ordered, rather than a goal he will pursue actively and independently.

2. **Lack of leadership.** Because he describes education as a passive experience ("will **bring me** success"), it's hard to imagine him contributing much to his classes or his college community. This suggests that he will not be a leader in the classroom (Fatal Mistake #4). If he was in class with a weak teacher or hesitant students, would he pitch in or would he just complain? Does he have a commitment to contributing to the experience of his classmates, or is he just out for himself?

3. **Exclusivity.** His opening sentence emphasizes his sense of entitlement to a special place in an elite school: "At **my** highly regarded private school . . ." This suggests he may take excessive pride in being privileged. In other words, this is a warning sign of exclusivity (Fatal Mistake #9). The impression of elitism gets worse when he talks about going to a "**superior** college," which suggests that in his mind, schools (and people too?) are divided into the superior and the inferior. If these are the terms in which he sees the world, would he participate fully in the life of a diverse school?

4. **Seeming like a threat.** He describes his high school experience this way: "I am being prepared **to excel** . . ." Admissions people always get concerned by students who seem too focused on excelling or "being the best." If this is a student's sole motivation, rather than innate love of learning, they wonder, then how far will that student go to reach his goals? If he is overly competitive, will he steal from the library? Cheat outright on exams and papers? Destroy other students' work? Probably not, but by defining himself in blatantly competitive and even aggressive

terms, this student suggests he might pose a threat (Fatal Mistake #5) to other students and to the school.

5. **Lack of intellectual passion.** Describing his goal as excelling at a "superior" school, he suggests that his focus is on his class rank and not on what he learns. Notice what he's *not* saying here: He has no particular subjects he wants to study, and in fact hardly seems to notice that he's applying to a college, an institution dedicated to learning. He appears to lack intellectual passion (Fatal Mistake #3). What would this person be like to teach or to study with? Would he have any real interest in his courses, any true intellectual passion? Or would he be demanding and arrogant with his professors and fellow students, especially, perhaps, if he judges them to be less than "superior"? Ask yourself: Would *you* want to be his teacher? Join his study group?

6. **Social insensitivity.** His description of the life path he expects for himself, moving from a "highly regarded" school to a "superior college" and then on to "success and happiness," implies a very limited view of how people lead their lives. It hints at a lack of moral imagination (Fatal Mistake #6), the ability to imagine a world where some top students can't afford the top-ranked schools, or have to stay near to family to help them get along, or simply find success and happiness without moving from one high-prestige situation to another. There is a whole world of experience out there, and these words suggest a limited frame of reference that could make him a less successful student and a more difficult "fellow citizen" of the school.

7. **Selfishness.** His emphasis on his own **"success and happiness"** seems to say that all he really wants out of college is self-promotion and personal gain. For some admissions people, that one word, *success*, on its own will cast images of selfishness

and greed. Of course, just about everyone hopes for material success, but in a personal statement, it's not enough to "just be yourself." In fact, it can be fatal to imply that even your "best self" is merely self-serving and hungry for personal comforts (Fatal Mistake #2). "Success" might be a goal you can state in an application to business school, but it's one of the most dangerous words you can use in an arts-and-sciences application. And aside from this one word, the impression of selfishness is intensified by his passive view of education. He seems interested only in what a school can do for him, and not in what he can do for his school.

Now that you've worked through this book, you know how to recognize the thirteen fatal mistakes that can keep you out of the school that would be best for you. You also know that your application is a chance to show the sides of you that will help colleges see how you would fit in at their school. In the two appendices that follow, I recap my suggestions for working on the essays and the interviews. If need be, you can refer back to the chapters again as you work.

By now, you know that college admissions people care about character. This theme was summed up well in a graduation address that I've never forgotten. Looking down at the Andovder student body from his podium, head of school Ted Sizer said to his graduates, "We have given you the intellectual tools and personal experience in your time here for you to continue to achieve, and to succeed in a competitive world. But"—dramatic pause—"have we made you generous?"

As you now know, college admissions people care about character. They care because they are usually very decent people themselves, and they see their job as creating a college community of good people. So although they value intellect and talent, and pay careful attention to test scores and grades, when they consider students of comparable talent and accomplishment, in competition with each other, they look for good character. Show them the best you've got and I trust that you will find a school that's a great match for you.

ACKNOWLEDGMENTS

Thanks to the generous and original sponsors of Dunbar Educational Consultants: Dudley and Susan Dumaine and Charlie and Ellen Collis.

To Robert Cummings, our ingenious and indefatigable president.

John Greenwood, the most knowledgeable consultant for athletes in the country, and a most prolific college visitor.

Ned Bigelow, the greatly esteemed and loved head of our Boston office.

Emilie Hinman, a careful researcher and caring, astute consultant.

Nancy Edmiston, our brilliant, highly respected counselor for MBA and law candidates.

Gloria Choy, the talented, hospitable, and dedicated head of our Hong Kong office.

Henry Choy, an astute and perceptive consultant and pediatrician in Hong Kong, who (based on student essays he's seen) gave the book its original title, *Application Suicide.*

Rick Dickson, a greatly revered school and therapeutic placement person, whose multiple talents enhance the resources and abilities of our team.

Jean Wolf, the savvy head of our Paris office, who also works out of Washington, D.C.

Susan Jones, the resourceful, versatile consultant who advises students from preschool to career out of Washington, D.C.

Will Goodman, MBA, who invariably offers keen insight to students and their parents.

Caroline Brokaw Tucker, MBA, whom I call "Super Star" because she contributes powerfully to every phase of our operation.

Roe Blanchard, an able counselor who works mainly with our *Boston Globe* students, as we are the official college counselors for all the children of *Boston Globe* employees.

Juana Barrios, a multilingual and gifted consultant, who represents us in Los Angeles.

Cammie Bertram, who served us with great ability and professionalism for eight years.

Our former counselors in the old Brookline office, Nancy Pfiffer, Tink Davis, and Susan Wolman, all of whom served our students with extraordinary ability and caring. And to Susan Goudail, our scholarly and dedicated counselor in pre-Katrina New Orleans.

Former mentors: Andover's legendary college counselor, Marion Finbury, and the highly respected independent consultants Mimi Lewis and out of Groton, Frank and Muffin O'Brien. Thanks also to my closest St. Paul's colleague and renowned writer of over twenty books on the English language, Richard Lederer.

Our support staff—past and present: Joanne Bovey, Lisa Nelson, Martha Ross, Barbara Burns, Lisa Walker, Di Di Woodhull, and Brenda Vanecek.

Business advisors: the late Aubrey Jones; Kevin Gumper, Esq.; David Feldman; Mike Delaketo; Tom Drumm; and accountants Linda Levesque and Gary Clayton.

Special thanks to G. F. Lichtenberg for his formatting and organization and his uncanny ability to make a book flow. Also, thanks to those involved in early editing, Susan Latour and Will Goodman.

And to Jessica Sindler of Penguin Books, Gotham, for pacing us and contributing to the book's refinement.

Thanks to my great agent, Robert Diforio, and to Bob Runk, an author who unselfishly put us together.

And congratulations to our discoverer, Erin Moore of Penguin Books, Gotham.

Writing the Essay

Essays can take a lot of time—but in the end it's worth it. So start early, if possible right after junior year ends. Commit to one work session a week and start brainstorming ideas for the personal essay. How? Give yourself time to try out any topics that seem interesting, anything at all, for now. Just sit down once a week and put down any ideas you have, good and bad, serious and silly. Talk to anyone you feel comfortable with about what you might like to write about. Make lists, draw pictures, anything you like. For now, you really can "just be yourself."

Once you have a number of ideas, you can start to think about which of them would interest your readers. Admissions people are hoping to learn what distinguishes you from other applicants, what you're like when you're most mature and intellectually passionate. Ask yourself: Which of your various essay ideas demonstrates your best self and might help them to see you in a good light? What topic might interest someone who doesn't know you personally?

One way to choose among possible essay topics is to ask yourself whether any of them will help to show admissions people the character traits that interest them the most in a candidate. Look for topics that let you show off one or more of these traits:

Intellectual passion: The enthusiasm, interest, personal knowledge, and curiosity you bring to your academic interests

Commitment to your community: Your enthusiasm for contributing to your school community, whether in or out of class

Moral imagination and inclusivity: Your ability to show empathy and your gift for building bridges with dissimilar people

It's not necessary to find a topic that demonstrates all of these traits—one of them, memorably shown, can be enough. Nor should you try to argue or explain why you think you have these traits. It's no help, for example, to say something like "The best example of what a hugely empathetic person I am came a few years ago . . ." That only seems naïve, or worse, arrogant. Admissions people know what they're looking for, and if it's in your essay, they'll notice. Pick a topic that will give them the chance to see one of these traits in you, and then concentrate on the specifics of your essay.

Once you have a draft that feels solid to you, check it for these fatal mistakes:

Selfishness: Have you gone beyond your personal story and interests to find a universal topic that will help readers connect with you?

The Threat of Aggression: Have you made sure not to put others down as a way to build yourself up? Have you made it clear that although you may be highly motivated and ambitious, you don't always need to be the best?

Dependency: Are you hiding behind the opinions and support of others, or are you showing your own independent preferences and thought?

Negativity: Have you limited the negative as much as possible, making sure to emphasize what you are enthusiastic about?

Failure to learn from rough times: If you have chosen to write about hard times or mistakes, remember that they want to see how resilient you were in your response, and how your judgment developed as a result of the experience.

Finally, make sure to give yourself plenty of time to revise. In my experience, it takes a few tries to come up with an idea you really like, a few more tries to figure out what you want to say and how you can move from the personal to the universal, and some more time to come up with a conclusion.

When you work on the conclusion, be on the lookout for narrow thinking. Make sure to:

Acknowledge that there is more than one side to any argument you may be making.

Develop your universal topic to try to push through to a conclusion that reflects your own abstract idea.

Once you have a polished draft of your essay, you'll want to get feedback from a select reader or two whom you trust, perhaps a parent and a teacher who knows you well, and then you'll need some help neatening it up at the end. If by the end you haven't revised at least four times, you probably aren't showing colleges the best you can do.

ESSAY TIPS

1. Try to plan and start all your essays and even short-answer questions well ahead of deadlines, and follow this approach for them all.

2. Read the directions very carefully, paying close attention to the questions and to the suggested length.

3. Begin by writing a few rough drafts and then set them aside for a few days.

4. Read your rough drafts aloud to family members or friends, or record yourself reading them so you can hear how they come across out loud.

5. After each revision, check carefully for spelling and grammatical errors, unnecessary words, and poor sentence structure.

6. Polish your essay and again listen to how it sounds. Keep in mind that your essay could be read aloud to an admissions committee.

7. Type your essay, if possible, unless the college requires a handwritten version, and make a copy for your files.

8. Double-space the lines of the essay to make it easier to read.

9. Don't wait until the last minute. The best essays are written over time.

10. Have fun. Really! Of course there will be times you feel nervous or pressured, but look for opportunities to enjoy your work.

APPENDIX B

Preparing for the Interview

Again, it's a good idea to start preparing early. Interview practice sessions are a great way to generate ideas not just for interviews but for essays, so I encourage you to try your first sessions the summer before your senior year, when you're starting to work on your personal essay. The best college interviews are the ones that give your interviewer a feel for what matters to you, what motivates you, and what sort of college student you are likely to be, all in the course of a comfortable, unforced conversation. But how do you prepare for an unrehearsed chat? To begin, take some time to get comfortable with the interview format. Set up a room with two chairs and maybe a desk in between, and have a friend or parent "interview" you for thirty to forty-five minutes. Assign your interviewer a particular college to represent, and ask him or her to think of a few questions specific to that college. The interviewer can start by asking some of the general questions that are typical:

Tell me about yourself.

Why are you interested in our school?

What are your strengths and weaknesses as a student?

Do you like your high school?

If you could start high school over again, would you do anything differently?

What has been your most positive experience in high school?

Describe your favorite teacher.

What is your favorite class or subject?

Tell me about a paper or class assignment that you found particularly stimulating.

Tell me about a time when you were faced with a setback and you overcame it.

If you could make a difference in the world, what would you do and why?

What do you want to study in college and why?

How do you spend your free time?

Which of your extracurricular activities has been most satisfying?

What did you do last summer?

How do you contribute to your school or community?

What other colleges are you considering?

What are some of the criteria you are considering in selecting a college?

It may take a few practice sessions to start to feel comfortable. You'll know you're getting comfortable when you begin to enjoy answering these questions, at least a little. Enjoying it may seem unimportant, but it's actually crucial because the more you are able to relax and enjoy the interview, the more you can be yourself, and the more the interviewer will feel he or she is meeting a genuine and interesting person.

Of course, as you now know from reading this book, it's not enough just to be yourself. You also need to be selective about what parts of yourself you want to share in the brief time you have. After you've had a comfortable practice session, take some time to review what you talked about and to notice when you seemed to warm up. Which questions seemed to leave you most energized, confident, and caring? When were you your most mature and engaged? The subjects you talked about at those times are good topics for you. They give you the chance to answer the questions that admissions people have in mind:

What do you feel passionate about? What do you love to learn about?

What kinds of leadership come naturally to you, whether at the head of a group or one-on-one, in class, in extracurriculars, or in casual social situations?

What experiences with people or places have you had that surprised you, engaged you, or helped to change your thinking? These might be times you were able to build a bridge to connect with other people you met, or connections you made through your empathy and imagination.

And in case the interviewer doesn't ask the questions that you are expecting to lead to these subjects that you're passionate about, be sure to prepare your own thoughtful questions that will allow you to touch on these subjects.

As you identify topics you like to talk about, you will probably find that you wish you could remember more specifics. For this reason, before your next round of practice and again before real interviews, take time to refresh your memory:

Find and reread some of the schoolwork you are most proud of, or the kinds of schoolwork you prefer to do when you have a choice, so you can give your interviewer specific examples of the schoolwork that interests you most.

Look over books, magazines, or Web sites that especially interested you when you read them, so you can talk about what they said and why they mattered to you. Make a point of noting to yourself who wrote them.

Look over the school's course catalog and online materials, and if possible walk through the campus and talk to students before your interview, so you can make it clear to your interviewer that you care enough to learn about the school.

Prepare a few questions you might like to ask about the college. Go beyond factual inquiries like "How many computer science majors are there?" and draw on your interviewer's experience with the school with questions like "With separate campuses for science majors and liberal arts majors, are there chances for the whole school to come together?"

Consider your weak spots, the fatal mistakes you know by now that you are most apt to make, based on your reading of this book. These will very likely come up in your practice interviews, so when you review a practice session, ask your practice interviewer about whether you slipped into any of these:

- Selfishness: Talking about your experiences and your wishes to the exclusion of anything else, including the interest of your interviewer.

- Conversational "skimming": zipping from one thought to another. If you're prone to skimming, try having your practice interviewer reply "Tell me more about that" to every answer you give, once or even a few times. Soon you'll start hearing that voice in your head, encouraging you to get below the surface.

- Narrow thinking (part one): If you find yourself adopting a strong position on a controversial issue, take time to acknowledge that the issue has at least two sides, that you are familiar with them, and that you can see some merit in a view different from yours.

- Narrow thinking (part two): Be willing to go from a personal experience or gripe to a group or universal concern.

- Dependence on the ideas of others: If you are prone to rely on other people's opinions, remember that interviewers are interested in hearing what you think. They don't care if your opinion is "right," as long as they see you have the curiosity and the courage to try to think for yourself under pressure. From my point of view, that's what a college education is all about.

- Going negative: Be careful not to let unhappy stories snowball. You may need to practice moving through the difficult stuff and emphasizing instead what you've accomplished. (If you find yourself going negative, review the Cure for Negativity in Chapter Eight, on "Going Negative.")

- Exclusivity: If all of the events and experiences you describe involve one narrow group of people, you may give the impression of being unable to build bridges. Look for opportunities to talk about a range of different relationships that demonstrate your openness and connection to people different from yourself.

INTERVIEW TIPS

1. Schedule your interviews with admissions offices well ahead of time. If possible, start in June at the end of your junior year.

2. Read the college's catalog ahead of time. Know what interests you about the school.

3. Arrive on time. Dress neatly, cleanly, and respectfully.

4. Greet the interviewer with a firm handshake. Make eye contact.

5. Remember that first impressions are very powerful, so be sure to start off with something positive to say. You might go in knowing a few things you are very positive about, so you can look at your interviewer's first question as a chance to talk about one of those.

6. Bring energy to the interview and try to enjoy your interviewer. The interview is an exchange of information and reflection, and it is also a personal encounter. Try to be natural, relaxed, and responsive. Don't be afraid to laugh and enjoy yourself.

7. Keep making eye contact from time to time during the interview.

8. Don't worry if the interview doesn't cover your life's history or your school record; the admissions office will receive all the objective information it needs. The point of the interview is to give the interviewer a chance to see how maturely you think and how interesting you are as a person. By preparing thoughtful questions, you can make certain that the focus is on your strengths and interests and that you have given the college serious thought.

AFTER THE INTERVIEW: FOLLOW UP!

After your visit, write a note to thank your interviewer for an interesting and/or informative session and to demonstrate your continued interest in the college:

- Be specific about something that will remind the interviewer about you:

  - A common interest you shared, such as a book or movie you talked about.
  - A talent of yours.
  - Something the interviewer said about the college that gave you greater insight into the student body, academic program, etc.

- Refer to something you like about the college that you were not aware of before your visit.

- If you visited a classroom or a professor or a department, mention what you learned from the visit.

HOW IMPORTANT ARE INTERVIEWS?

Admissions committees use interviews not just to evaluate applicants, but also to promote their institutions and to help applicants make good choices about which schools would suit them. The significance of personal interviews for admission varies with each college. By itself, an interview will generally neither admit nor reject you, but it may be a pivotal factor. Interviews are a chance for you to gain an advocate for your application and also to establish a point of contact in case you have questions later.

Don Dunbar is a former college admissions counselor for Phillips Academy, Andover, and he is one of the nation's premier experts on the college admissions process. His career in education spans more than thirty years and he has served as teacher, chaplain, coach, guidance counselor, and admissions consultant for public and private schools in the United States and abroad. In 1984 he founded Dunbar Educational Consultants, one of the largest and most successful firms of its kind, which has helped clients gain acceptance to over two hundred prestigious schools, including all of America's top colleges and universities. Don lives in Fairfield, Connecticut.